# POETIC VOYAGES
# CAMBRIDGESHIRE

Edited by Helen Chatwin

First published in Great Britain in 2001 by
*YOUNG WRITERS*
Remus House,
Coltsfoot Drive,
Peterborough, PE2 9JX
Telephone (01733) 890066

HB ISBN 0 75433 114 8
SB ISBN 0 75433 115 6

# FOREWORD

Young Writers was established in 1991 with the aim to promote creative writing in children, to make reading and writing poetry fun.

This year once again, proved to be a tremendous success with over 88,000 entries received nationwide.

The Poetic Voyages competition has shown us the high standard of work and effort that children are capable of today. It is a reflection of the teaching skills in schools, the enthusiasm and creativity they have injected into their pupils shines clearly within this anthology.

The task of selecting poems was therefore a difficult one but nevertheless, an enjoyable experience. We hope you are as pleased with the final selection in *Poetic Voyages Cambridgeshire* as we are.

# CONTENTS

Glebelands Primary School
| | |
|---|---|
| Melissa E Taylor | 1 |
| Stacey Smith | 1 |
| Alexander Platt | 2 |
| Phillippe Aichinger | 2 |
| Charlotte Butler | 3 |
| Hazel Thulborn | 3 |
| Leanne Dennis | 4 |
| Hannah Van Koppenhagen | 5 |
| Peter Fletcher | 6 |
| Natasha King | 6 |
| Laura Swingler | 7 |
| Christian Smith | 7 |
| Victoria Bailey | 8 |
| Leanne Barson | 8 |
| Sharon Smith | 9 |
| Ashley Young | 10 |
| Kelsey Jenkins | 10 |
| Katie Stephens | 11 |
| Megan Mawdsley | 12 |
| Erwin Nooteboom | 13 |
| Oliver Fox | 13 |
| David Bainsfair | 14 |
| Sophie Louise Hockley | 14 |
| Elizabeth Bailey | 15 |
| Grace Firth | 16 |
| Katie Sharp | 16 |
| Liam Smith | 17 |
| Alice Moden | 17 |
| James Bainsfair | 18 |
| Scott McEvoy | 18 |
| Daniel Brown | 19 |
| Jack-Charles Gabriel | 20 |
| Emily Dixon | 20 |
| Chloe Aichinger | 21 |

| | |
|---|---|
| Aaron Smith | 22 |
| Charis Abraham | 22 |
| Alexandra Cooper | 23 |
| John Paul Stevenson | 24 |
| Sophie Phoenix | 24 |
| Dawn Gleaves | 25 |
| Kerri Smith | 26 |
| Ryan Constable | 26 |
| Adam Elliott | 27 |
| Kimberley Woolfenden | 28 |
| Kimberley Tyers | 28 |
| Ashleigh Sellen | 29 |
| Zekeriya Keskin | 30 |
| Jillian Honnor | 30 |
| Holly Gladwin | 31 |
| Charlie Dawson | 31 |
| Lewis Jenkins | 32 |
| Jordan Pretlove | 32 |
| Aaron Perry | 33 |
| Keeley Hardman | 34 |
| Alana Cornhill | 35 |
| Carrie Wallis | 35 |
| Kelly Stephens | 36 |
| Lewis Furr | 36 |
| James Hamence | 37 |
| Matthew Ward | 37 |
| Jessica Dean | 38 |
| Max Kelly | 39 |
| Carl Constable | 39 |
| Oliver Smith | 40 |
| Joshua Armstrong | 40 |
| Charlotte Wool | 41 |
| Zoe Knight | 41 |
| Charlotte Phoenix | 42 |
| Nathan Fletcher | 42 |
| Dale Tabbitt | 43 |
| Graham Briscoe | 43 |
| Philippa Woolfenden | 44 |

| | |
|---|---|
| Laura Osbourn | 44 |
| Olivia Parnell | 45 |
| Gemma Ayling | 45 |
| Gareth Stracey | 46 |
| Leila Harrison | 46 |
| Jacob Taylor | 47 |

**King Edward Junior School**

| | |
|---|---|
| Michael Shaw | 47 |
| Sarah Wright | 48 |
| Aedan Ridley | 48 |
| Laura Frith | 49 |
| Joanne Beaney | 49 |
| Claire Langman | 50 |
| Samantha Payne | 50 |
| Carl Turpie | 51 |
| Laura Jayne Cooper | 52 |
| Aimee Everest | 52 |
| Jared Stephenson | 53 |
| James McDermott | 53 |
| Katie Manchett | 54 |
| Laurie Hughes | 54 |
| Kayleigh Sparkes | 55 |
| Rebekah Dunstan | 55 |
| Justine Langman | 56 |
| Charlie McKenzie Stewart | 56 |
| Jessica Aldred | 57 |
| Clarrisa Robertson | 58 |
| Lucy Matthews | 58 |
| Hannah Matthews | 59 |
| Amber Howie | 59 |
| Thomas Salisbury | 60 |
| Luke Roscoe | 60 |
| Daniel Hill | 61 |
| Sophie Church | 61 |
| Sarah Cornwell | 62 |
| Damien Harris | 62 |
| Bethany Iliffe | 63 |

| | |
|---|---|
| Nathan Malik | 63 |
| Heather Long | 64 |
| Jasmin Keen | 64 |
| Lauren Pettitt | 64 |
| Carl Flippance | 65 |
| Emma Hayter | 65 |
| Danny Arnold | 65 |
| Lydia Easey | 66 |
| Rebecca Waters | 66 |
| Matthew Busby | 67 |
| Kayleigh Peacock | 67 |
| Rebekah Turpie | 68 |
| Timothy H Milner | 68 |
| Calum Thompson | 69 |
| Emily Edgley | 69 |
| James Cartwright | 70 |
| Charlotte Rex | 70 |
| Emily Henderson | 71 |
| Matthew Brown | 71 |
| Hayley Hills | 72 |
| Lauren Buddle | 72 |
| Jack Manning | 73 |
| Jordan Palmer | 73 |
| Rebecca Stephenson | 74 |
| Hannah Skerrett | 74 |
| Bethan Lenton | 75 |
| James Blackwell | 75 |
| Sophie Morton | 76 |
| Alex Gillett | 76 |
| Melanie Flack | 77 |
| Kayleigh Henshaw | 77 |
| Samuel Earley | 78 |
| Sarah Furnell | 78 |
| Becky Cowles | 79 |
| Stewart Coleman | 79 |
| Deanne Peacock | 80 |
| Chloe Chapman | 80 |
| Lucy Melton | 81 |

| David Colwill | 81 |
| Louise Edgley | 82 |
| Jonathan Rigby | 82 |
| Declan Heady | 83 |
| Niomi Gill | 83 |
| Antonia Elise Butcher | 84 |
| Kelly Long | 84 |
| Lee-Ann Watson | 85 |
| Leilani Rabemananjara | 85 |
| Roiss McQuaid | 86 |
| Emma Furness | 86 |
| Geraldine Fleming | 87 |
| Katie Richardson | 87 |

## Manea Community Primary School

| Sarah Snow | 88 |
| Tiffany Hollingsworth | 88 |

## Mepal And Witcham School

| Luke Collet-Fenson | 89 |
| Emma Hayes | 90 |
| Rory Martin | 90 |
| Christie Watson | 90 |
| Paul Goodman | 91 |
| Leanne Cole | 91 |
| Gemma Chamberlain | 91 |
| Sam Smith | 92 |
| Luke Baker | 92 |
| Rose Elizabeth Rowell | 92 |
| Blake Sanders | 93 |
| Andrew Horsfall | 93 |
| Soffia Handley | 93 |
| Richard Day | 94 |
| Daniel Duffy | 94 |
| Jodi Leigh Rayner | 95 |
| Syringa Fox | 95 |
| Krystal Sturman | 96 |
| Ben Somers | 96 |

| | | |
|---|---|---|
| | Amber Rutterford | 97 |
| | Charlotte Collet-Fenson | 98 |
| | Alexandra Baldwin | 98 |
| | Nicola Housden | 99 |
| | Jordan Houghton | 99 |
| | Leanne Alice Jeffrey | 100 |

## Milton CE School

| | | |
|---|---|---|
| | Philip E Bailey | 100 |
| | Michael Ellum | 101 |
| | Ruby Weeks | 101 |
| | Hannah Hill | 102 |
| | Shona Forge | 102 |
| | Jacob Wisbey | 103 |
| | Thomas Western | 104 |
| | Emily McDonald | 104 |
| | James Ostler | 105 |
| | Emma Murphy | 106 |
| | Stephen Bargh | 106 |

## Murrow Primary School

| | | |
|---|---|---|
| | Karen Cunningham | 107 |
| | Steven Lee | 107 |
| | Andy Cunningham | 108 |
| | Emma Harris | 108 |
| | Helen Halton | 109 |
| | Ashley Virgo | 109 |
| | Amy Morris | 110 |
| | Petra Blackwell | 110 |
| | Zoe Hennells | 111 |
| | Sarah Skinner | 112 |
| | Lee Heath | 112 |
| | Ashley Green | 113 |
| | Craig Brown | 113 |

## The Rackham CE Primary School

| | | |
|---|---|---|
| | Edward Middleton | 114 |
| | Lucie Potter | 114 |

Jennifer Ludman 115
Rachel Seymour 115
Lynsey Jones 116
Natalie Szulc 117
Sabrina Woollard 118
Katharine Hardman 118
Ashleigh Witt 119
Emily Richardson 119
Anna Wallis & Katharine Hardman 120
Jacqueline Hedges 120
Catherine Ascough 121
Chantle Oakes 121
Jade Whitmore 122
Chloe Elms 122
Matthew Parish 123
Lucy Kinna 123
Roger Goetze 124
Hayden Watson-Stewart 124
Emmeline Holt 125
Jake Caffrey 125
Michael Chapman 126

The Weatheralls Primary School
Joshua Blyth 126
Rebecca Blyth 127

# The Poems

## MY PET COOKIE

My pal Cookie is brown and white
he's very shy and he likes the dark.
He has a friend called Elmo
and he had a friend in Oscar
who loved to run around with his
bro Monty. They looked so sweet
all huddled in a group. Sadly they're
dead now and have gone to sleep.

Cookie had a fight over a tube,
this was not his fault though.
Walk through the gate
stop, and listen. Squeak, squeak,
squeak from the hutch Cookies
saying 'Don't forget me!'
My pal Cookie is brown and white.

*Melissa E Taylor  (11)*
*Glebelands Primary School*

## CATS

Cats, cute, cuddly little things, I've got two
cute little things they would not hurt
a fly, just chase it a bit and chase mice away
and just fun to watch them play.
They both chase all kinds of things including
each other I love them to bits and
even some nights they come on my
bed and me and kitty would go to sleep.

*Stacey Smith  (9)*
*Glebelands Primary School*

## THE MASK OF MAJORAS

In the tomb
of peril and doom
where it's dark and stingy
damp and slimy
and the walls are limy.

It's where devils dwell
Werewolves howl,
bats fly, goblins die
and spirits cavort in draughty rooms

The key lies
where all the hunters have died.
sparkling and shiny.
Just waiting to suddenly be taken away
he still lies in the tomb of time
building life to one day *rise!*

*Alexander Platt (10)*
*Glebelands Primary School*


## THE CRYSTAL RIVER

The river finishes as a stream and turns into a
great big river. It travels for miles and miles
until it comes to its first waterfall.
Starts to get ferocious
You can see all the water bubbling
and hear it rubbing.
Soon it comes to its first meander
and then heads into another direction.
Soon it comes to an end and enters the sea
but the river will still go on for many years to come.

*Phillippe Aichinger (10)*
*Glebelands Primary School*

# THE FLAT

My dad wore a hat
In our old flat
This is my mum
She had lots of fun.

Todd was a boy
He had a special toy
We had a dog
Who liked the fog.

I had long hair
But my sister was unfair
She was fun
But sucked her thumb.

*Charlotte Butler (11)*
*Glebelands Primary School*

# SIMILES

The sparkly explosion
The colourful explosion
The brightest explosion
Smellier than garbage
Hotter than an oven
Smokier than a magician
Louder than a brass band
Bubblier than my bath
As boiling as roast potatoes just come
Out of the oven.

*Hazel Thulborn (7)*
*Glebelands Primary School*

## THE WIZ WAGER

There once was a thing called a Wiz Wager
Who came from outer space
He had a big dagger
He walked down Torrow Road.

He broke into my house
And stole my glass mole
Then he killed my pet mouse
And he ate it all.

I cried and cried
As he took me away
And I said 'I haven't lied'
But he took me on

We went into his spaceship
And as we went he drank a cup of tea
I said 'Can I have a sip!'
And it tasted horrible

When we go to a place called Nikle Nog
I yelled take me back
Then I saw a gigantic frog
And it took me for a ride

It took me to a cave
And it was pitch black
And the Wiz Wager gave me a wave
He scooped me up and put me on a table.

And then he said 'Eat up!'
When I looked at the table
There was a dead pup
And lots of other stuff

There was scribble wagers, funky jelly,
Golden curls, tissue sausages,
Net swirls, chocolate tea
And it fitted all in my belly

The next day he took me home
But it was a bit sad to say goodbye
He left me with a gnome
And I remember him well.

*Leanne Dennis  (10)*
*Glebelands Primary School*


## PRETTY KITTEN EXPLOSION

The potion was as sparkly as the stars
It tasted like the most delicious milkshake you've ever tasted
It sounded like tulips swaying in the breeze
The smell was the sweetest smell you ever smelt.

It was as whizzy as a firework
The colours were more colourful than a rainbow
The collar of the kitten was a lovely violet colour
A medallion saying 'Sparkle'

Her fur was glittery
Eyes as blue as the sea
Ears as pink as a rose
Her fur was white and ginger
With the brownest paws.

*Hannah Van Koppenhagen  (8)*
*Glebelands Primary School*

## CHEMICAL MIXTURE

In my dark damp lab
I am brewing a mixture.
With a drop of this and that
And a huge blob of this,
Kapow, wow an explosion.

It smells like a very smelly Viking, that
hasn't had a bath in weeks.
And sounds like a dying bird
It tastes as yucky as a bowl of rotting fish
And feels as gory as sheep's eyeballs
Dipped in jelly.

Ah, a bright swirl
Add a swish of this and that.
Kaboom! Another explosion
But this one is different, it is funny,
Hilarious, it is laughing
And it is the bubbliest mixture in the universe.

*Peter Fletcher  (8)*
*Glebelands Primary School*


## THE EXPLOSION

The explosion was
As smelly as a cheesy sock.
As sparkly as a firework exploding
As bubbly as a crocodile
As hot as a volcano exploding
The greatest explosion ever
*Bang!*

*Natasha King  (8)*
*Glebelands Primary School*

## PRINCESS RAINBOW CLOUDS

A princess whizzing like rockets,
Smelling like red, red roses
Tastes like a soft, strawberry sweet
Eyes as bright as the moon.

Glittery smoke more colourful than a rainbow,
Feels soft as silky fur,
Sounds like an innocent girl
Looks like a beautiful fairy.

Sparks brighter than the sun
Her dress lights up the dark.
Her voice like a choir
Beautiful red cheeks
The kindest princess in the world.

*Laura Swingler  (8)*
*Glebelands Primary School*


## MONSTER

My monster's eyes were as dark as mud puddles
His ears were bigger than elephant's ears
His teeth were sharper than crocodile's teeth
He tasted like orange soda
His skin was as spiky as a cactus
He smells of rotten food
The monster was uglier than a gooey alien
As gooey as gunge
As bright as the burning hot sun
The biggest monster in the world.

*Christian Smith  (8)*
*Glebelands Primary School*

## WITCHES' STEW

Witches' stew - witches' stew
Slimy bits and smelly green goo
Add an odd sock, a caterpillar
The whiskers from a blue Chinchilla
Slugs and snails and puppy dogs' tails
From girls take teeth and bitten nails
Witches' stew - witches' stew
Fit for a witch to chew

Witches' stew - witches' stew
Scares the likes of me and you
Mashed up moths and butterflies
Sticks and stones and old mud pies
It even has (I'm afraid to say)
Dead animals from Black Bay
Witches' stew - witches' stew
Fit for a witch to chew

Witches' stew - witches' stew
Has things from inside a loo
A used plaster, a sailor's hat
Petrol and a smelly cowpat
Stale bread works a treat
But do you know what's best to eat?
Witches' stew - witches' stew
What's missing is *you!*

*Victoria Bailey (9)*
*Glebelands Primary School*


## DOLPHINS

Dolphins are clever
Doing tricks all day.
Racing after boats
Chasing, tagging, rubbing coats.

As quick as a cheetah,
Swimming a metre.
Friendly as can be
Squeaking to each other all day long.

*Leanne Barson  (8)*
*Glebelands Primary School*


## CHEMICAL EXPLOSION

The pot went bang
Bright sparks flew out as colourful as a rainbow
It felt like squidgy eyeballs
And smelled like rotten fish.

It looks like buffaloes in the wild
Tasted like rotten bananas
Sounded like popping fireworks
More disgusting than soggy mud.

Quicker than a flash of lightning
Slimier than gunge
It looked like a warty witch
And was as bright as the shiny moon.

It was as loud as one hundred beating drums
As wobbly as a new born bird
As silly as a clown telling jokes
And as clumsy as a very big elephant.

As smelly as a rotten dustbin
As colourful as a rainbow
As weird as a nonsense poem.

*The scariest explosion*
*In the world!*

*Sharon Smith  (9)*
*Glebelands Primary School*

## PETS

Once I took my pet to the vet
While he was there he died.
So I asked my mum 'Can I buy a pet?'
Then we had a burger, fried.

Then I bought a fish
Then we had to leave
I looked at my fish while I was eating out
Of my dish.

Four days later the fish is dead
'Can I have a new pet?'
I said while staring at my favourite colour red.
Please Mum, I want a pet.

*Ashley Young (9)*
*Glebelands Primary School*


## THE EXCELLENT EXPLOSION

As the professor made his wonderful explosion
It was . . .
As sparkly as a firework blasting in the air,
Hotter than you being put in the oven!
Smellier than fish and chips sitting on your plate.
As runny as your tomato soup
When you just hate it,
It's the purplest and greenest liquid in the whole world
As bubbly as washing-up liquid in your sink.

The *biggest* explosion I've ever seen!

*Kelsey Jenkins (8)*
*Glebelands Primary School*

# THE PEACOCK

The peacock is a pretty sight,
Its feathers twinkle in the moonlight.
One day a parrot came down from a tree,
'Look at me!
I'm more beautiful than you!'
The peacock laughed and began to shout,
'Stupid parrot, sort yourself out!'
'Oh come on peacock, look at you!
Your feathers look like mouldy stew!'
'Don't you lie to me sweetheart,
For I have had enough!'
The peacock walked away in a huff.
'Let's see if I'm really that ugly!'
She looked at her reflection in the mirror,
She began to cry and shiver.
The parrot turned into a witch
'Look! Soon I'll also be rich.'
The peacock spat water at her
'No, no! My beautiful fur!'
She melted away to goo and slime.
Soon a handsome eagle came along
And sang Miss Peacock a beautiful song.
Only some fur left from the witch
Which they carried.
She threw it in the water
And her beauty was back again.

*Katie Stephens  (9)*
*Glebelands Primary School*

## THE WITCH

'Twas a dark and gloomy day
When a witch went out to stray
She took her cat
And her hat
To pick poisonous berries.

Later on that day
She strayed right back
With her cat
To her wooden shack.
Her heart was thumping with desire,
As she placed her cauldron on the fire,
And took the berries she had picked
She placed them in her hand,
They were as small as a grain of sand.

She tipped them in the cauldron
Without any care
And mixed them up, and mixed them up
With slimy frogs' eyes, as slimy as a snail
It started bubbling and steaming and
Glowing very bright.
And gave an amazing stare.
And all of a sudden
There was a bang,
And gave the witch a fright.

*Megan Mawdsley (8)*
*Glebelands Primary School*

# HANDSOME PRINCE

The explosion!
Clattered
And sparkled as bright as the sun!
But
It smelt like a field of roses,
And it felt as good as your best friend
And it looked as big as a rainbow.

It also tasted like a chocolate cake
As bright as a multicoloured firework
That's just been let off,
And peaceful like a mouse.

And it sounded like a bird singing
High in the tree.
Spinning around the room
Like a whizzy rocket!

The loudest explosion on Earth!

*Erwin Nooteboom  (9)*
*Glebelands Primary School*


# THE UGLY MIXTURE

The Professor was
As ugly as hat-back pig
As green as a gooey frog
Smellier than a bit of cheese
Softer than cotton wool
More dangerous than the crocodile
Smellier than a green alien
The smelliest mixture ever to be seen.

*Oliver Fox  (8)*
*Glebelands Primary School*

## THE GOBBLY GOO

The Gobbly Goo lurks by the loo
Waiting to strike for food.
He jumps up behind you and
takes a big bite of you until
there's nothing but dust.

The Gobbly Goo came out from
the loo crawling on his slimy tummy.
As quick as a flash
through the kitchen he dashed
to get to the living room.

The Gobbly Goo so quick and cool
that nobody noticed a thing.
With a growl and a roar he
was out the front door.
So the Gobbly Goo lurks by the
loo no more.

*David Bainsfair  (10)*
*Glebelands Primary School*


## THE MAGICIAN WHOSE TRICKS WENT WRONG

The magician's tricks always went wrong
Even though he practised all the day long
He tried some magic one day
But it didn't work out either way

He used a bone that was very old
Trying hard to make bars of gold
He forgot all the right words to say
And ended up with a huge pile of hay

He tried to pull a bunny from a hat
But all he got was a big fat rat!
His magic wand was all bent and broke
When he asked for wine, he got Coke!

The magician was really quite sad
Because his tricks were so very bad
So one day he decided to quit
As he was sick of being a *twit!*

**Sophie Louise Hockley  (10)**
**Glebelands Primary School**


## THE MAGNIFICENT MAXOME EXPLOSION

The magnificent maxome explosion is
As blue as the ocean
When at its calmest.
As fluid as still water
That no one has touched yet!

The magnificent maxome explosion is
As lovely smelling as perfume,
It's not quite hot but certainly not cold,
It's louder than a full-sized trumpet
As huge as the largest elephant!

The magnificent maxome explosion is
Smoother than a piece of metal
Melted into lead,
The softest explosion in the solar system
Is the *maxome!*

**Elizabeth Bailey  (8)**
**Glebelands Primary School**

# PROFESSOR GREENBOTTLE'S AMAZING EXPLOSION!

Professor Greenbottle's explosion was
As hot as the shining sun
on a sunny day,
As bright as an exploding firework
in a starry sky.
As blue as the afternoon sky
As huge as a giraffe's house.
As glittery as a gold star at night.
Smellier than cheesy socks under the bed,
The loudest explosion I've ever heard.
*Bang!*

*Grace Firth (9)*
*Glebelands Primary School*


# THE EXPLOSION

The explosion is as
smelly as some boiling,
colourful, twinkly potion
swirling round and round.
The pot was going chuckle,
chuckle, then it went
boom. As loud as a fireworks
boom, boom. It was as`
bright as some potion
going round, then it got
so loud.
Boom it went.

*Katie Sharp (9)*
*Glebelands Primary School*

## THE FASCINATING MIXTURE

Professor Liam's mixture was
As dangerous as a train crashing
And the people killing themselves.
Smokier than a fire in a building
And an elephant on top.
Greyer than a mouse
Rolling in grey muck.
Louder than a cow
Who feels sick.
A bigger explosion
Than a huge building falling down.
Professor Liam made the smokiest, loudest and
Greyest mixture ever.

*Liam Smith  (8)*
*Glebelands Primary School*


## CHEMICAL EXPLOSION

Mr and Mrs Chemical were doing a test
to see what happened to water and lava
it was bubbling, it crackled.
It was hot, slimy and smelly.

It was getting bigger like a whale,
then it went *bang!* And all the
liquid exploded.
It was bright, sparkly as a sequin
and was as loud as a cymbal!

Then they knew what to do
and did it all again.

*Alice Moden  (8)*
*Glebelands Primary School*

## THE MONSTER

One day was told
It was so cold
Christmas is near
I saw a reindeer

One day was mean
So ugly and green
A monster was near
It ate my reindeer

One day in May
Was spooky and grey
The monster came back
And had a snack

He was as big as an elephant
Bigger than a house
The biggest monster I ever
Did see.

I escaped in a flash
I hurried in a dash
The monster was scary
And so very hairy.

*James Bainsfair (8)*
*Glebelands Primary School*


## SCOTT'S CHEMICAL EXPLOSION

My chemical explosion
It smells like rotten eggs
And sounds like a lightning storm
It tastes like soap mixed with out-of-date chicken

*It's the biggest explosion in the world!*

It feels like a lion roaring at the top of a hill
It looks like a bonfire night
It smells like millions of smelly clothes
It's as gooey as a sewer!

*It's the brightest.*

*Scott McEvoy (7)*
*Glebelands Primary School*


## THE MONSTER

The monster was as smelly as a sewer that
hadn't been cleaned out in a month.
It tasted like mouldy jelly that had been left
in the fridge for a year.
It was as hot as a bonfire that had just gone
up in flames.
It looked like a massive tomato, as big as the
Eiffel Tower.
It was more multicoloured than a rainbow
It slithered across the floor like a snail
It felt like a mound of slime.
It even tasted more horrible than an
over-grown tomato.
It was greener than slime.
It was scarier than a vampire.
Its claws were sharper than daggers.
Its eyes were brighter than the sun
It was the soggiest thing I'd ever felt
It was as powerful as the wind
It had warts all over its body
It was as long as a snake
It was the smelliest thing I've ever smelt.

*Daniel Brown (8)*
*Glebelands Primary School*

# WIZZED POEM

Into my pot what can I put?
A red-speckled frog as red as a balloon
and pinky brains as slimy as a dinosaur.
Mix it up
see the contents, wiggle and squirm
getting warmer.
Hotter than lava, hotter than hot water
hotter than the sun.
*Explode!*

*Jack-Charles Gabriel (8)*
*Glebelands Primary School*


# THE CAT IN MY GARDEN

There's a cat
In my garden
I see every day
He's tame
And he's friendly
And loves to play
He's soft and funny
With a sweet meow
I like this kitten
As he tumbles about.

*Emily Dixon (10)*
*Glebelands Primary School*

## THE LOVELY WIZARD

'Twas all upon a gloomy day
A lovely wizard came to stay.
His head as big as a pumpkin
And his eyes are as big as four dumplings
'Twas all upon a gloomy day.

One day he came upon a winter's day
Then he went out for a stray
He took his wand, nat and his cat
And went out to pick this or that
One day he came upon a winter's day.

Then he came back from his trip,
With a very jolly skip.
He put his apples in his cauldron
By the fire
Then let his heart to desire.

Then he felt very hot,
As hot as a fire.
Then he went out for someone
To hire.

He bought an owl and another cat
Then he listened. *Boom* went
His cauldron. Then as he giggled
He said 'That's why I was getting hot!'

*Chloe Aichinger  (8)*
*Glebelands Primary School*

## PETS VS VETS

The dog's creating mayhem
he's knocked over the cage.
The budgie's gone loose
the cat's in a rage.

The vets have got their needles
creeping down the stairs.
What will be a surprise?
Getting hit by the mice with pairs!

The otters have gone in the water
Spitting water from the banks.
The vets are coming closer
they're acting like tanks!

The snake is good at biting,
going around the grass.
One fake move and its
poison will be a blast!

So you see they're squabbling.
It will be over soon, you'll see.
Over this problem about the otters asking
*'Will you marry me?'*

**Aaron Smith  (9)**
**Glebelands Primary School**


## DOGGY

Doggy, doggy, waggle your tail
Catch the ball without fail
As funny as a clown
Who's falling, falling down

*Doggy*

Running, chasing. *Bang!*
Gone to the pedigree gang.
They run, they chase
They have a pretty face.

*Dog! Dogs!*

**Charis Abraham  (8)**
**Glebelands Primary School**

# CATS

All through the night
The moon is shining bright
and all I can hear is the meowing of cats.

*Cats*

Lots of cats go to the vets
To have a check-up
miaowing, miaowing, purring, purring.

*Cats*

Cats have their dinner
Meat chunks, jelly chunks
Cats like a long nap

*Cats*

Cats eyes are as bright as the moon
I run outside soon
To see all the cats flash with a boom

Cats fur is as furry as fur
Cats eyes are as bright as
Lights glowing in the dark

*Cats*

**Alexandra Cooper  (7)**
**Glebelands Primary School**

## SCIENCE

Who would understand science
Definitely not me
For whenever I do science
My face goes red to see

Who would understand science
Not me I say
Because we do science
Every single day.

Who would understand science
We mostly do it in May.
We wait until the bell goes
So we can go out to play.

Who would understand science
I drift off to sea
Who would understand science
Definitely not me.

*John Paul Stevenson (10)*
*Glebelands Primary School*


## THE MAGNIFICENT MIXTURE

My mixture is:
As dangerous as a long violin
In your eye
Purpler than an eye
Punched out in a battle
Sparklier than gold shiny glitter
Smellier th an a pig's barn
That hasn't been cleaned out for over 5 years.

As exciting as a holiday coming in a weeks time,
As explosive as a sizzling bomb
That blows up the solar system.
As massive as a tall building
With five storeys
As gooey as an alien with grass for his hair.
The biggest mixture I've ever made
*Bang!*

*Sophie Phoenix  (8)*
*Glebelands Primary School*


## MONKEY BABIES

Don't leave your baby monkeys sitting in the swamp
A crocodile might eat him up, crump, crump, crump.

Don't leave your baby monkey sitting on a track
A lion might be coming, snack, snack, snack.

Don't leave your baby monkey sitting under a tree.
A snack might wrap him up, swish, swish, swish.

Don't leave your baby monkey far away loose,
A mad man might be running shouting 'Moose! Moose! Moose!'

Watch your baby monkey wherever he goes
A rat might step on its toes, toes, toes.

Don't let your baby monkey sit in the park
A dog might have bit him, bark, bark, bark.

Don't let your baby monkey play like Bart in the show,
Because you just know what's going to happen,
You know, know, know!

Leave your baby monkey sitting in a tree
Feed him on bananas and pick out his fleas.

*Dawn Gleaves  (10)*
*Glebelands Primary School*

## THE BUBBLING EXPLOSION

The Professor's amazing explosion was
Hotter than a summer in Turkey.
As bright as a shining star
As dangerous as a hot cooker.
Jogging around the park
As gooey as gunge, green and blue.
As slimy as a frog from the water
As green as grass
That has just had a wash.
Smellier than a rat and a mouse
Bubblier than a witch's recipe
In the park
As scary as a monster
That has a large tongue
One of the gooiest potions I have ever seen!
              *Boom!*

*Kerri Smith  (8)*
*Glebelands Primary School*


## THE BIG EXPLOSION

As colourful as a rainbow
Feels squidgier than a slug
Tastes like rotten chicken
The loudest explosion in the street.

As rotten as an unripe tomato
Smells like a filthy pig
Louder than a drum
The squidgiest explosion ever.

Greener than slime
Smells worse than a bonfire
More disgusting than a black apple
The smelliest explosion the Professor made.

Gooier than a snail
Yellower than a banana
Greener than an alien from outer space
The gooiest explosion in the world.

*Ryan Constable  (8)*
*Glebelands Primary School*


# MR AND MRS TROUBLE'S BABY

Mr and Mrs Trouble's baby
is uglier than his grandad's belly.

He is green with no eyes
which is lucky because they
would look like pies.

His brown hair
is more disgusting than a bear.

He eats all the grub
and won't go in a tub.

So run from Mr and Mrs Trouble's baby
because if you upset him he will give a party.

PS If you really want to know he is older now
but looking more like a cow.

*Adam Elliott  (8)*
*Glebelands Primary School*

## MY CHEMICAL EXPLOSION

My chemical explosion is as
powerful as a warty witch.
Green as a spiky crocodile
As colourful as the greatest fireworks.
As smelly as grey smoke
As slimy as gunge
As wet as green grass.

It smells like squashed tomato
As disgusting as a rotten banana
My chemical explosion
Is like a baby crying,
As bright as the blazing hot sun
As big as when a boy throws
A ball up in the air.
As mean as a snake
The fastest explosion in town!

*Kimberley Woolfenden (7)*
*Glebelands Primary School*


## MY RABBIT DROOPY

My rabbit Droopy is
Cute, black and fluffy
He's smelly, fat and big
I love my rabbit Droopy.

My rabbit Droopy he
Follows a sock
Thumps when he marks his territory
Lays on my bed.
I love my rabbit Droopy.

My rabbit Droopy
When he washes his nose it looks really cute
He eats white chocolate
I love my rabbit Droopy, I do, I do.

*Kimberley Tyers  (9)*
*Glebelands Primary School*


## MY CHEMICAL EXPLOSION

My chemical explosion is
As powerful as a warty-witch.
As green as a spiky crocodile
As colourful as great firework.
As smelly as grey smoke
As slimy as gunge.
And as wet as green grass.

It feels like squashed tomatoes
As disgusting as a rotten banana.
As wobbly as jelly
It sounds like popping fireworks
And is as bobbly as bobbles
It looks like a colourful rainbow.

The explosion went all over me
It turned me into a monster
I growled like a spotty leopard
With the longest tail.

I looked like a giant
I smelt like a rotten tomato
And was as colourful as some fireworks
I was the gooiest in the world.

*Ashleigh Sellen  (8)*
*Glebelands Primary School*

## THE TERRIBLE MIXTURE

The mad scientist's mixture was
As slimy as a toad covered in gunge,
As smelly as cheesy socks and rotten eggs
Left in the sewers for five years.
As dangerous as a fire
In a paper house.
As hot as the sun
In ten ovens.
Spicier than five chillies
Covered in black pepper.
As green as a gooey green frog
Rolling in grass.
More revolting than the ugliest thing
I've ever seen.

*Zekeriya Keskin (9)*
*Glebelands Primary School*


## THE AMAZING MIXTURE

As green as an ugly monster
Like the grass.
As smelly as a rabbit
As soft as a sofa
That has comfy pillows
As dangerous as a wolf
That eats ten people
The gooiest mix ever to be made.

*Jillian Honnor (8)*
*Glebelands Primary School*

## AT THE VETS

A budgie's in for toenail clipping
Pecks the vet on the nose
Dogs in for booster injections
Sits on the vet's toes.

Cat needs dental check-up
Bites the vet upon the hand.
Mousey has a poorly tail
He doesn't understand.

Hamster's got an overgrown tooth
Tugs at the vet's finger.
A rabbit jumps under a cupboard
Thinks he'll stay and linger.

With all this excitement
The vet jumps out the window
He runs off down the path
Shouting 'I'm going home!'

*Holly Gladwin  (10)*
*Glebelands Primary School*


## THE GREAT SCIENTIFIC EXPLOSION

The professor's scientific explosion was
Gooier than a slimy alien
From outside space
Greener than an ugly monster
Smellier than a pair of old, mouldy socks
Sparklier than a shining star
The brilliant explosion ever to be seen on this planet.

*Charlie Dawson  (8)*
*Glebelands Primary School*

## DON'T WORRY!

When you're in the battlefield you will be
One of two things,
Injured or not injured.
If you're not injured, don't worry
But if you are, your injury will be
One of two things.
Serious or minor,
If it's minor, don't worry.
But if it's serious, then
One of two things will happen to you.
You'll live or you'll die
If you live, don't worry
But if you die, *you can't worry!*

*Lewis Jenkins (10)*
*Glebelands Primary School*

## EXPLOSION

My chemical explosion!
It smells like rotten eggs
And sounds like lightning!
It tastes like soap mixed with out-of-date chicken!

*It's the biggest explosion in the world!*

My chemical explosion
It showered colours like a rainbow in a stormy sky
It feels like an earthquake is shaking you.

*Jordan Pretlove (7)*
*Glebelands Primary School*

# I HAVE A FRIEND

I have a friend called Spike
Who went on a hike
With his bike
And went down a dike.

I have a friend called Snoddle
Who had quite a wobble
He met a duck
That had quite a buck.

I have a friend called Diddle
He went for a long piddle.
He had a dog called Boo
Who drank from the loo.

I have a friend called Max
Who liked to relax.
One day on the sofa
He saw a rather big lofa.

I have a friend called Fred
Who liked to stay in bed.
One day in bed
He bumped his head.

I have a friend called Phil
Who had a very long bill
He went to pay
Then he got kicked away.

*Aaron Perry (10)*
*Glebelands Primary School*

## MY LITTLE DOGGY

There was a doggy
Sitting on a hoggy
All alone.

Down the stairs, the little doggy came
When the doggy needs a walk
I always take the doggy
Down the park.

I always put the doggy
On my knee
When I'm on the swing
Or going down a slide.

Whenever I let her go in the garden
She always finds the froggy from next door.

My doggy always comes on my bed to keep me company
I always give my doggy a kiss
Before I go to school or to the shops.

She always cares about me
When I'm gone, she never forgets me
Not even when I'm gone for two hours.

We will always be near each other
Even when I am in London.
We will always be best mates
In the whole world
We both love each other.

*Keeley Hardman  (10)*
*Glebelands Primary School*

## THE COOL EXPLOSION

The Professor's dangerous potion was
As powerful as a vicious vampire slayer
As dangerous as a red-eyed hairy monster
As jumpy as the forest kangaroo.
As smelly as breath, smelling sheep's wool.
More gooier than a monster that's slithered in a ghost drain
that hasn't been cleaned out.
As green as a monster
Sitting on the grass.
As glittery as a shimmering gold star
As squidgy as a blue and purple alien
Standing in an Alien's room.
The biggest explosion ever to be seen.
        *Boom!*

*Alana Cornhill (9)*
*Glebelands Primary School*


## THE AMAZING MIXTURE

The Professor's mixture was
As green as an ugly frog.
As soft as a really nice dog
As dangerous as a big bad wolf.
As slimy as a silly alien
As gooey as a fat big fish.
The biggest mixture that
I have seen.

*Carrie Wallis (7)*
*Glebelands Primary School*

## Nonsense Poem About Animals

Once there was a duck
Who lived in a truck,
The duck got stuck
With the old ducks.

Once there was a cat
Who was talking with a rat,
The rat loved the cat
The cat loved the rat.

Once there was a dog
Who was sleeping on a log.
The sing-song flowers were singing
The church bells were ringing
Whilst the dog was asleep.

There was a pig
Who was really *big*.
He liked to wriggle
When he slept.

*Kelly Stephens (9)*
*Glebelands Primary School*


## The Ugly Mixture

The Professor's mixture was
As smelly as a pot-bellied pig.
As green as a wet crocodile
As gooey as a hungry frog
As slimy as a slippery alien
The smelliest mixture ever to be seen.

*Lewis Furr (8)*
*Glebelands Primary School*

## CATS

Cats, cats they are black
All day they fight
They climb up trees and fall from a great height.

At night they come inside
Cats, cats they are hairy.
Cats! What would we do without them?

Cats, cats they are black
All day they sit on a mat.
When they go out they fight rats.

*James Hamence  (10)*
*Glebelands Primary School*


## THE EXPLOSION

The explosion is
Redder than blood.
As revolting as sick
As hot as a volcano.
As sparkling as a bomb
Bubblier than a cake baking
As slimy as a slimy fish
It's the best explosion
I have ever seen!

*Matthew Ward  (7)*
*Glebelands Primary School*

## CHOCOLATE

Chocolate, chocolate
I love chocolate
Repeat the words after me

I love chocolate
You love chocolate
We love chocolate
That's okay!

Have a chocolate ice cream
Have a chocolate bath.
Have a chocolate pudding
And make it last.

Eat it hot and
Eat it cold
Eat it in a pile of mould.

Now can you
See I am just
So easy to please
By eating a bar today.

Put some nuts on
Put it in a crab
Put it in the loo
And eat it fast.

I love chocolate, don't you?

*Jessica Dean  (10)*
*Glebelands Primary School*

## WHO INVENTED SCHOOL?

Who ever invented school
I'd like to meet them today?
Because you would never ever ever imagine
How much they would pay!

They don't know what we've been through
They don't have any idea.
They don't know what our teacher's like
Cos she's really really weird.

Do you think they invented lessons
The boring ones you know.
The ones where no one listens
The ones where no one knows!

Who invented books
The books that teachers read
The really old history books
The ones that no one needs.

*Max Kelly  (10)*
*Glebelands Primary School*


## PAUL

There was a young boy called Paul
Who was no use at football,
He kicked his own striker
Three dogs and a biker.
The only thing he missed
Was the ball.

*Carl Constable  (10)*
*Glebelands Primary School*

## THE ROBOTIC MONSTER

Once there was a monster, big and brown,
No hair and skin, he was a robot thing,
With four legs that were heavy
And bendable *big* arms
And ten eyes wriggly and wavy.
He was very tired so he hipped and
He hopped and had a sleep.
Ten hours he was planning
But he made a fuss
With the neighbour's puss
That made noises all night.
The monster said
'Shut up!'
And the cat hid in the mat.

*Oliver Smith  (9)*
*Glebelands Primary School*


## THE ROCK EXPLOSION

The Professor's rock explosion was
As ugly as a big ugly monster
As green as a dangerous green drink
As smelly as old cheesy socks
Slimier than a big slimy frog
The slimiest frog I have ever seen.

*Joshua Armstrong  (8)*
*Glebelands Primary School*

## My Chemical Explosion

The explosion exploded
It was as sparkly as sparklers
It tasted as disgusting as mud
It was louder than a volcano
As slimy as gunge
And scarier than a ghost.

My explosion exploded
As colourful as a rainbow
It's smellier than a baby's bottom
As powerful as a motorbike.
The biggest bang in the world!

*Charlotte Wool (7)*
*Glebelands Primary School*


## Chemical Explosion

There was a big explosion one day
When children came out to play.
It was sizzling
Then it started fizzing
It was crackling again
Then it all came.

The explosion was as big as an elephant
Bigger than a plane.
The biggest explosion ever!
They said
'Now it's time for bed.'

*Zoe Knight (9)*
*Glebelands Primary School*

# LITTLE SIS

There's a sound in the cupboard,
A sound down the loo,
A sound in the old school yard
Whatever shall I do?

Once the sound had stopped,
I curled up in my bed,
But it started again,
And I nearly lost my head!

So I got out of my bed,
And I opened my room door,
The sound was unbearable,
'Though I didn't ask for more.

I found out what the sound was,
Although I flinched a bit,
It wasn't as bad as I thought it would be,
It was just my little sis!

*Charlotte Phoenix (11)*
*Glebelands Primary School*


# DISAPPEARING GHOST

A ghost came into my room last night
And came across, what a terrible fright!

I screamed so loud it broke the glass,
It blew Mum's ears off with a blast!

The ghost then went and we were happy,
Nanna said 'Go tell your pappy.'

*Nathan Fletcher (8)*
*Glebelands Primary School*

## STRIPPERS

If you fall in a river of piranhas
they will strip off your flesh
there will be no time for screaming
there will be no time for groans
because in forty-five seconds
you're nothing but bones
so just stay out of their way or
you will surely pay.

We all like a feed, I just hope
that he will fall in so we can get
dinner so we can be on our way.

But that's what you think, you silly fish,
if I wanted to I could put you on my dish, fish!

*Dale Tabbitt (9)*
*Glebelands Primary School*


## CHEMICAL EXPLOSION!

What can I put in my pot?
Grey brains as smelly as socks.
Frog's eye as blue as a balloon.
Mix it up
Mix it up
Bits of chemicals bubbling up
With a *boom* and a *bang*
It started to glow,
And there he was.

*Graham Briscoe (9)*
*Glebelands Primary School*

## THE LITTLE CAT

There was a little cat
Who always stayed in a hat
She always caught a rat
One day she could not find a rat
Again she could not find one
And she got as small as an ant
Smaller than a grain of sand
The smallest cat I ever did see
A year later she disappeared
Because she did not catch a rat again.

*Philippa Woolfenden (7)*
*Glebelands Primary School*

## THE BIG EXPLOSION

'Twas all upon a sunny day,
I looked around then picked up my pot,
And in my pot I put,
Spiders as hairy as monsters.

Water as wet as the sea
Then gave it a big stir
Then I put in a cat's purr
It was bubbling and the pot was shaking

Then *bang!*

*Laura Osbourn (7)*
*Glebelands Primary School*

## CHEMICAL EXPLOSION

It has eyes as dark as mud.
Its nails are like elephants' horns.
Skin as spiky as a hedgehog.
It smells like rotten food.
It sounds like popping fireworks.
As big as a giant.

Teeth like razor-sharp swords.
As dirty as a muddy puddle.
As ugly as a witch.
As smelly as a rotten drainpipe.
As green as a dirty river.
Hair like nasty worms.
It gets muddier every time.

The biggest explosion in the world.

*Olivia Parnell (7)*
*Glebelands Primary School*


## THE AMAZING POTION

The amazing potion was . . .
More purple than a slimy monster
Squashier than a carton of orange juice
Gooier than sticky chewing gum
Flowing over the top of the cauldron
Uglier than a frog, *bang!*

*Gemma Ayling (8)*
*Glebelands Primary School*

## WRESTLING

There once was a man in the ring,
Who heard the bell go ding,
He wished it was over,
The first time he fell over.

The champion gave him a can of whoop-ass,
The poor guy hoped the feeling would suddenly pass
He got a kick and a punch,
And hoped it was lunch.

Then the tides turned,
And the champion's thighs burned.
With a kick and a stunner,
He made the champion say 'Bummer.'

The wrestling guy won,
And the champion was gone.
The man said 'I'll now soak in brine,
. . . And from 'wrestling', I think I'll resign.'

*Gareth Stracey (10)*
*Glebelands Primary School*


## THE EXPLOSION

It was as gooey as melting chocolate
It was like a bonfire
It was as hot as a volcano
Bigger than you would ever believe
It was as lumpy as custard
It was the gooiest explosion
You would ever see.

*Leila Harrison (8)*
*Glebelands Primary School*

## THE ALIEN

Once there was an alien
as big as Mars.
His ears were big and red
and he'd got seventeen bubbly legs.
He'd got a little spaceship
as little as an ant.
He'd got seventeen spiky arms.
He was as big as the moon
and he had fifteen squinty eyes
and one more thing, he acted like a cow.

*Jacob Taylor  (9)*
*Glebelands Primary School*

## POEM

'I'm taking the dog out'
'Why?'
'Because he needs the toilet'
'Why?'
'Why do you keep saying 'Why?'
'Why'
'I'm taking the dog out now'
'Why?'
'Bedtime'
'What!'

*Michael Shaw  (10)*
*King Edward Junior School*

## FREEDOM OF BIRDS

Up in the sky so clear and blue
The birds are flying, oh so high
With their wings they are gliding by
To the trees
Where they sit and sing
On a lovely sunny day
Big ones keep little ones away
From the food and drink
Put out in the garden sink
Big ones go, little ones come
In their lovely colours
On their breasts and wings
To clear what has been left.

*Sarah Wright (10)*
*King Edward School*

## PYRAMID

Huge, colossal
Dangerous, many
People have fallen off
Inside they are full of
Hieroglyphics and sarcophagi
Of pharaohs who ruled Ancient
Egypt.

*Aedan Ridley (9)*
*King Edward Junior School*

## BEST FRIENDS

Best friends are the best,
They always make you smile.
Everyone's got a best friend,
They always stick up for you.

I have a best friend,
She is a genius
I'm always with her.
My mum always
Says 'You two are
    stuck together like glue.'

*PS They are excellent.*

*Laura Frith (9)*
*King Edward Junior School*


## MY SISTERS

My sisters and I
We play like friends.
My sisters and I
We fight like cats.
My sisters and I
We share our games.
My sisters and I
    Together.

*Joanne Beaney (10)*
*King Edward Junior School*

## THE STAFFROOM

Teachers having a snooze,
Dreaming about cup cakes.
'Not fair!'

Giving each other nudges,
Breathing chocolate breath,
Because of too many chocolate fudges,
'Do you think I should tell?

No, I'll get into too much trouble,
Uh, oh! I think they've spotted me!
See you later!'

*Claire Langman (8)*
*King Edward Junior School*


## A BIRD IN THE SKY

As I stand in a field looking around,
I feel content with the silent sound,
Until a bird appears from above,
With a song so sweet, you'd swear it was a dove.
Gracefully gliding across the sky,
I think to myself, 'Oh why, oh why
Can't I be that bird up in the sky?
Why can't I glide and be free, oh why?'

*Samantha Payne (11)*
*King Edward Junior School*

# TELEVISION

Television's your friend
You call him TV
You play with him every day.

He can be bright and dull,
Happy and sad,
Even sporty and relaxed.

He's seen everybody
The Queen and Britney Spears
Also Steven Redgrave and S Club 7.

He's heard every song
'Reach', 'Thriller' and even '2 In A Million'
Also the National Anthem and Bob the Builder.

He's seen every city
London and Washington,
Cambridge and Chicago.

He's touched every sight
Big Ben and the Eiffel Tower
Also Tower Bridge.

He's smelt every smell
Open sea and rare oil
Also fresh money and animals' nests.

He's tasted every food
Squid and ostrich
Also chips.

Television's your friend
You call him TV
You play with him every day.

*Carl Turpie (10)*
*King Edward Junior School*

## MY PARROT

My parrot is a different colour
He is
    Red
    Green
    Blue
    Yellow

He has white wings with black spots

He has golden feet and black nails
He likes to say 'Who's a pretty boy then?'
Sometimes he asks people questions
My pet parrot
He is
    Really
    Really
    Really

    *Cool!*

***Laura Jayne Cooper (8)***
***King Edward Junior School***


## MY SNOWMAN

My snowman is white
My snowman is bright
My snowman has a carrot nose
My snowman has a pop star's pose
I think my snowman's cool
With a scarf made of wool.

***Aimee Everest (8)***
***King Edward Junior School***

## CATERPILLAR, CATERPILLAR

Caterpillar, caterpillar
Munching on a leaf
Munch, munch
All day long.

Cocoon, cocoon
Hanging on a leaf
Wriggle, wriggle
Wriggle, wriggle
All day long

Butterfly, butterfly
Flying in the air
Flap, flap
Flap, flap
All day long.

*Jared Stephenson (9)*
*King Edward Junior School*


## MY PET HAMSTER

My pet hamster
Comes out when it is dark
He shuffles in his cage
He sucks on his bottle of water
He is munching on his food
When it comes 6 o'clock
He will scramble to his comfortable bed
When it comes 7.30 again
He will be on his paws again.

*James McDermott (8)*
*King Edward Junior School*

## THE WEIRD TEA PARTY

At half-past nine, we had some tea.
We wondered what it was,
We went to the table, it was all gone,
We wondered where it was.
Mum said, 'We'll still have a gay time.'
We kept on cooking, it kept on going,
We went under the table,
The invisible man wondered where it was
Mum and Dad and the children were under the table,
The invisible man set off in tears
He went to another tea party.
The whole family had a gay time
        At half-past nine.

*Katie Manchett  (8)*
*King Edward Junior School*


## HAVE YOU EVER WONDERED?

Have you ever wondered where teachers go after school?
I have.
I wonder if they go to space and hang their socks on the moon?
I wonder if they go to Egypt and get a curse from the mummies?
I wonder if they go to the swimming pool and turn into sharks?
The thing is, I don't know,
So I think I'll follow one home today
Then I'll find out.

*Laurie Hughes  (8)*
*King Edward Junior School*

## CHRISTMAS LIGHTS

Red, yellow, green
Orange, blue, pink
All so joyful
All so wonderful
Off in day
On at night
All so joyful
All so wonderful.

Purple, white, cream
Cold, silver, bronze
All so joyful
All so wonderful
Lovely to see
Beautiful to look at
All so joyful
All so wonderful.

*Kayleigh Sparkes (8)*
*King Edward Junior School*


## FRIENDS

Friends are hard to find,
They play with me and others,
They are there when I am glad,
They are there when I am sad,
They are always there when you need them
What would we do without *friends?*

*Rebekah Dunstan (9)*
*King Edward Junior School*

# A DAY AT THE ZOO

One day I went to the zoo
And saw a monkey.
It was perched on a perch
Eating a green banana.

One day I went to the zoo
And saw an elephant.
It was wallowing in a pool of mud
Then it walked around with a great big thud!

One day I went to the zoo
And saw a lion.
It was roaring at the top of its voice
Its shaggy mane shaking.

One day I went to the zoo
And saw a dolphin.
It was splashing around in the water
Its skin glistening in the sunlight.

One day I went to the zoo
And saw a kangaroo.
It was jumping all around,
Its baby in its pouch.

*Justine Langman (9)*
*King Edward Junior School*


# SHOWERS AND BATHS

I love showers
A dreamy, steamy, hot shower
The water dripping down
Steamy, dreamy, hot shower
I love a steamy, dreamy, hot shower.

I also love a deep, steamy, dreamy, hot bath
Sinking into Wonderland,
Imagining anything,
I feel as droopy as a tired, old baby,
I love a dreamy, steamy, hot, deep bath.

*Charlie McKenzie Stewart (8)*
*King Edward Junior School*


## ANIMALS

Animals are cute,
Some are very furry.
I cuddle them as if they're teddy bears.
Some have scaly skin.
Horses are very tall,
They gallop very fast
I want one of my own.
Zebras are black and white.
Reptiles have scaly skin like a crocodile,
Elephants are huge and very heavy,
They like squirting water at each other.
Butterflies are different colours,
I like purple, blue and other colours that
Fade to make a beautiful butterfly.
Dolphins are very smooth,
They leap around in deep oceans,
The only time people see them is out in boats
Birds are beautiful, you get different kinds,
Robins, kestrels, blackbirds and sparrows
Kangaroos leap about, they have pouches
                    to hold their born.
Bees buzz around collecting pollen.
I think animals are very cute creatures.

*Jessica Aldred (9)*
*King Edward Junior School*

# WHY?

'I'm just going to the shop'
'Why?'
'Because I need some bread'
'Why?'
'Be quiet'
'Why?'
'I'm leaving now'
'Why?'
'Because if not the shop will be closed'
'Why? Why? Why?'
'Go to bed'
'Why?'
'Because I said so!'

*Clarrisa Robertson (9)*
*King Edward Junior School*


# MY DREAM HORSE

My dream horse will be beautiful,
She will be black.
Maybe she will win every race!
She won't be lazy.
I shall play all day out in the countryside,
I love her even though she is not real.
That's my dream horse Jemma!
She will jump very high,
She will be greatly loved
She will always be mine.

*Lucy Matthews (8)*
*King Edward Junior School*

## THE TEACHER WHO DID

On the day Tutankhamun came to my party,
when he got on the bouncy castle his mask came off
and his bandages flopped off.

On the day a mummy came to stay, he went to sit down
but he couldn't sit because his legs weren't bandaged up right.

On the day a Pharaoh came to tea, his head came off and
landed in a plate of man-eating snakes.

On the day Miss Dunster came to tea, her legs flopped off.

*Hannah Matthews (7)*
*King Edward Junior School*


## SUMMER

Summer is a great time of year
But we know autumn is near,
Children play by the lake
Building dams are what they make,
I like the summer breeze through my hair
And the smell of the fresh air.
Summer is a great time of year
Children have enjoyable times
But autumn is near,
Children tell stories and rhymes.

*Amber Howie (9)*
*King Edward Junior School*

## THE ANCIENT EGYPTIAN MUMMY

On the day a mummy came to tea,
He caught his bandages on the shelf.

On the day a mummy came to tea,
He crashed into a lovely tree.

On the day a mummy came to tea,
He tripped over the step.

On the day a mummy came to tea,
He fell into the fish pond.

On the day a mummy came to tea,
He slipped on some soap and fell right in the bin,

On the day a mummy came to tea,
He drank a lot of tea.

On the day a mummy came to tea.

*Thomas Salisbury (8)*
*King Edward Junior School*


## MONSTERS

M  ashing metal
O  verpowering
N  asty teeth
S  ome are slimy
T  hrashing comets
E  xtremely powerful
R  oaring with anger
S  lashing trees.

*Luke Roscoe (8)*
*King Edward Junior School*

## BRITAIN

Great Britain is the best.
Really it is better than the rest.
Egypt, Italy, France, we're better than them
And nobody can beat us.
The British are the best, better than the rest.

Better than China, New Zealand, Australia,
Really they are not as good,
In teams we have to be,
Together we are better,
And nobody can beat us,
Nobody could beat us and nobody will.

*Daniel Hill (9)*
*King Edward Junior School*


## THE MELTING SNOWMAN

Kids, like us, like to build snowmen,
But kids don't like
To go out in the wintry white snow,
Because children are cold from head to toe.
Sometimes the children are sorry
For the snowmen when they melt.
Because they get sad,
And mean and bad!
So children hate it when they melt.

*Sophie Church (8)*
*King Edward Junior School*

## AN OLD MAN

There once was an old man,
Who had a very nice van,
He went for a drive,
And had a dive,
On a really hot day.

A man came along,
Singing an awful song,
With one ear,
Holding a tear,
On a cold day.

He tripped on a stone,
And broke a bone,
Fell down a gutter,
Which gave him a great flutter,
That was the end of the old man.

*Sarah Cornwell (10)*
*King Edward Junior School*


## ANGER

Anger is an evil beast
With his red body, green eyes and goat legs.
His claws, razor-sharp, ready to curse you with hatred and anger
Anger is invisible, that's why he strikes without warning.
Anger is the demon.

*Damien Harris (10)*
*King Edward Junior School*

## COMPUTERS

Computers can be fast,
Computers can be slow,
Computers are clever
There's nothing they don't know.

Some people like computers,
Some people don't
Sometimes they're right
But mainly they're wrong.

Computers never work,
They're always breaking down
Nobody needs computers
They drive you mad.

'Double-click on this,'
My teacher's saying
It's driving me insane
Nobody needs computers,
Especially not me!

*Bethany Iliffe (10)*
*King Edward Junior School*


## RHYME

Coconuts, coconuts, in the trees
Coconuts, coconuts, hanging from my knees
Water, water, all around
Water, water, in the ground
Water, water, in the air
Water, water, everywhere.

*Nathan Malik (9)*
*King Edward Junior School*

## SUPERSTAR

My dinner lady's a superstar, famous in the town,
She is always on television dancing up and down
She plays the bass guitar, she has hair down to her knees
She ties it back when she serves the mushy peas.
She has a private jet and a swimming pool
That's where she makes the custard
        before she comes to school.

*Heather Long  (9)*
*King Edward Junior School*


## SPRING

The little lamb
Sitting happily underneath those trees
In that horrible, nasty, wet, cold breeze.
*Look out! Look out!*
Can't you see spring is here,
But *look out! Look out!*
Summer is so near.

*Jasmin Keen  (9)*
*King Edward Junior School*


## BLUE

My favourite colour is blue,
It's beautiful for me and you.
Blue is the colour of the sky,
Blue is sometimes the colour of a butterfly.
Big, bold, beautiful blue,
I love you.

*Lauren Pettitt  (9)*
*King Edward Junior School*

## CROCODILE CAME TO TEA

On the day Crocodile came to tea,
He fell down the stairs,
Broke his tail,
Nurse Joy said 'Get away.'
When Nurse Joy went to check on Crocodile
He ate Nurse Joy
On the day Crocodile came to tea.

*Carl Flippance (8)*
*King Edward Junior School*


## ON THE DAY H CAME TO STAY WITH ME

One day someone came to stay for a year, it was H,
I showed him a bathroom,
I showed him the backyard,
He liked my brothers,
He played with the Sega,
I got annoyed with H,
The day someone came to stay for a year, it was H.

*Emma Hayter (9)*
*King Edward Junior School*


## A MUMMY

On the day a mummy came to tea,
He got his bandages stuck in the door.
He ate his tea, his hand slipped in the cream.
He went upstairs and his head fell in the loo.

On the day a mummy came to tea.

*Danny Arnold (7)*
*King Edward Junior School*

## SPRINGTIME

Springtime is here again
Icy snow on the ground
People enjoying the sun
Rivers flowing in time with fish
Growing flowers popping out of the ground
Nine lambs having children
Tulips growing in the fields
I feel as happy as a bird singing
The flowers and I all love the spring
Everybody enjoys springtime.

*Lydia Easey  (9)*
*King Edward Junior School*


## ANIMALS

Animals are very cute,
Cats and dogs are pets.
Squirrels are wild and sit in trees.
Eating acorns of course.
Penguins live in the cold.
Camels live in the heat.
Bears go and fish in rivers.
Birds sleep in twig nests.

*Rebecca Waters  (8)*
*King Edward Junior School*

## WINTER

The cold icy roads
The snowy blizzards blow.
Me on my out-back garden hill.
The snow is light and bright.
My sledge is blue and the sliding is fun.
The snowman comes, I lick an ice pole
It is cold.
Snowball fights, you get wet.

Falling snow.

Unknown caves to find.

Nice snow

*Fun!*

*Matthew Busby  (8)*
*King Edward Junior School*


## THE SNOWMAN

One winter day
I went out to play
The snow was glistening
The children were listening
I built a snowman
But sooner or later
He'd *gone!*

*Kayleigh Peacock  (9)*
*King Edward Junior School*

## WHY?

'I'm going out'
'Why?'
'To feed the rabbit'
'Why?'
'Because it wants something to eat!'
'Why?'
'Because it's time to feed her'
'Why?'
'I wish you'd stop saying why'
'Why?'
'Fiddledy hiddledy de why!'
'What?'

*Rebekah Turpie  (7)*
*King Edward Junior School*


## ON THE DAY THE MUMMY CAME TO TEA

On the day the mummy came to tea,
He met me,
He couldn't bear it, he needed a wee,
At half-past eleven,
He went up to Heaven,
On the day the mummy came to tea.

*Timothy H Milner  (8)*
*King Edward Junior School*

## WHAT?

'Good morning'
'What?'
'Do you want breakfast?'
'What?'
'Are you going out?'
'What?'
'It's a miserable day'
'What?'
'Stop saying what!'
'What?'
'Are you going to school on the bus tomorrow?'
'What?'
'Stop it!'
'What?'

*Calum Thompson (9)*
*King Edward Junior School*


## MUMMY ON THE RUN

A
Mummy
In a tomb
A Pharaoh on the move
Nile flooding quickly
The mummy awakes!
Click, click, click
The head lifts up
*Mummy on the run!*

*Emily Edgley (9)*
*King Edward Junior School*

## WHY?

'I'm just going to feed the rabbit.'
'Why?'
'Because it's hungry.'
'Why?'
'I need to.'
'Why?'
'I don't want him to starve.'
'Why?'
'How would you like it?'
'Why?'
'Why won't you stop saying why?'
'Why?'
'Because I have to.'
'Why?'
'I need to.'
'Want to clean him out and give him a drink.'
'What?'
'At last he said something else.'

*James Cartwright (8)*
*King Edward Junior School*


## THE DAY A MUMMY CAME TO TEA

On the day a mummy came to tea,
His bandages got trapped in the door,
They had strawberry jelly,
He loved it so much he ate it all,
His hands got stuck to the wall
While he was taking in his plate.

*Charlotte Rex (8)*
*King Edward Junior School*

## AUTUMN

Autumn days when the sky is blue,
The leaves fall from the trees.
They're orange and red,
Brown and yellow,
That's what I like to see.
As they fall from the sky,
They float, dance and sway,
As I stamp on them
They are crunchy and crispy
And they crumble on the ground.
I like to play with the leaves.
As I play with them I shiver
And they gently fall
    Down
       and
         Down.
It is very good,
As I walk I see leaves tumble down.
They tumble, twirl and dance
In the air
As the wind blows.

*Emily Henderson (7)*
*King Edward Junior School*


## ON THE DAY THE SNAKE CAME TO TEA

On the day the snake came to tea, it slithered through
a crack in the door,
On the day the snake came to tea, it ate the wobbly
jelly and then the snake wobbled,
Then it saw the ice cream and ate it and suddenly the snake
was frozen solid.

*Matthew Brown (8)*
*King Edward Junior School*

## MY MUM AND MY BROTHER

*My mum*

She is a lovely lady
She cooks the tea
She does my room just for me
She plays games with me
I love her because she always helps me.

*My brother*

He is very sweet
He loves to eat
He cries a lot
But that does not matter, he is only a baby
But I love him because he is the best.

*Hayley Hills  (9)*
*King Edward Junior School*


## THE DAY THE DINOSAUR CAME TO TEA

The day the dinosaur came to tea
He got his tail stuck in the door,
He tried to get out,
But he broke the door.
The day the dinosaur came to tea,
He swished his tail and broke the windows.
The day the dinosaur came to tea,
He put my mum's glasses on,
And chucked them in the bin.

*Lauren Buddle  (7)*
*King Edward Junior School*

## MY CATS

I have two funny cats
They think boards are surfing boards
Their names are Butler and Taylor
Taylor runs up and down ten times
And jumps on my bed like a hippopotamus
                    jumping on my bed
Butler is the one who plays with your feet
Taylor likes to sleep with you
Butler likes to eat
Taylor likes to explore
Butler runs about
Taylor climbs up shelves
Taylor and Butler like to hide.

> *Really, really, really*
> *funny!*

*Jack Manning (8)*
*King Edward Junior School*


## MUMMY'S FIRST TEA

On the day a mummy came to tea,
He walked through the door,
He fell on the stone stairs,
His bandages were undoing,
When he was eating, his head came off,
And fell down the toilet,
And the mummy could not see anything.

On the day a mummy came to tea.

*Jordan Palmer (8)*
*King Edward Junior School*

## MY CROCODILE GOES TO SCHOOL

On the day a crocodile came to school with me,
When I got there, he had already eaten the teacher,
He decided to eat the class dinosaur,
The headmaster came in and told us off but we did not care,
We just had fun and we went home early,
The next day my crocodile ate all the teachers,
And we had a party,
And my headmaster ran away from town and we
                    never saw him again.

*Rebecca Stephenson  (8)*
*King Edward Junior School*


## MY PIGS

'I am going out for a moment,'
'Why?'
'Because I need to feed the pigs,'
'Why?'
'It's their feeding time,'
'Why?'
'It's our dinner too,'
'Why?'
'Because'
'Because - oh can you just stop saying why'
'Why, well just stop saying why.'

*Hannah Skerrett  (7)*
*King Edward Junior School*

## WHEN A MUMMY CAME TO TEA

On the day a mummy came to tea,
He came straight through our door,
When he sat down, his arm fell off,
On the day a mummy came to tea,
Some of the bandages went into the teapot.
When my mummy had a drink of tea,
She saw some bandages in her tea,
My mummy told off the mummy,
He put his head instead of his bum in the toilet,
On the day a mummy came to tea.

*Bethan Lenton (8)*
*King Edward Junior School*


## FISHES

I like fishes,
When I'm cleaning the dishes,
My fish plays around the castle,
I call him a rascal,
When he goes to the treasure,
He has an adventure,
When he played dead,
I went to bed,
The next morning he died,
I cried.

*James Blackwell (9)*
*King Edward Junior School*

## WHY?

'Why do I have to go to school?'
'Because you do!'
'Why?'

'So that you can learn.'
'Why?'
'Because if you don't you will not learn!'
'Why?'
'If you don't go to school you will not be popular.'
'Why?'
'I am going outside now?'
'Why? Why?'
'Why? Why?'
'I have had it up to here.'
'Why?'
'Just go to bed.'
'What!'

*Sophie Morton (8)*
*King Edward Junior School*

## THE HUNGRY COCKROACH

On the day a giant cockroach came to school,
He ate my desk,
He ate my chair.
At playtime he ate the football,
He thought it was made of cheese,
On the day a giant cockroach came to school.

*Alex Gillett (8)*
*King Edward Junior School*

## WHY?

'Mum, I'm going outside.'
'Why?'
'Because it's hot.'
'Why?'
'Because I've got to meet my friend.'
'Why?'
'Because I'm not allowed to go round hers.'
'Why?'
'Because her mum said.'
'Why?'
'Stop saying 'Why?''
'What?'

*Melanie Flack  (9)*
*King Edward Junior School*


## MY IDEAL TEATIME

On the day S Club 7 came to tea,
We had ice cream and jelly babies,
When the cat ran out in front of them,
Bradley tripped over her and fell into
the ice cream pot.
After lunch I had permission to go to
the park with S Club 7.
On the day S Club 7 came to tea.

*Kayleigh Henshaw  (8)*
*King Edward Junior School*

# WHY?

'I need to cook a enormous dinner'
'Why?'
'Because it is tea time and I am hungry'
'Why?'
'Because I can do that'
'Why?'
'Because I'm going to and if you don't stop saying why I will shout'
'Why do aeroplanes fly?'
What did you say
'Why oh-o, ouch!'
'Bark' the dog said.

*Samuel Earley (8)*
*King Edward Junior School*

# ON THE DAY I TOOK MY KOALA TO SCHOOL

On the day I took my koala to school,
She went into class, made a mess,
She was too fast,
I just got her so I put her in my classroom
I got her some dinner, she ate it all up,
On the day I took my koala to school.

*Sarah Furnell (8)*
*King Edward Junior School*

## ON THE DAY A MUMMY CAME TO TEA

On the day a mummy came to tea,
He fell over a step and broke his leg in half.
His eyeballs popped in his soup.
On the day a mummy came to tea,
He drank some milk which came out of his neck.
His head popped in the teapot.
On the day a mummy came to tea,
He went to the toilet, half of his bandages went down it.
His hand got stuck in the freezer.

*Becky Cowles (8)*
*King Edward Junior School*

## KEEP ROLLING

I roll,
I love to roll,
I roll to school,
All my friends say I'm mad.
Sometimes when I roll to school
I hit lamp posts and trees
        and more trees
                and more trees.
When I get to school, I feel
                *dizzy.*

*Stewart Coleman (8)*
*King Edward Junior School*

## ON THE NIGHT

On the night the mummy came to the Hallowe'en party,
His hand got stuck on the washing line,
We pulled him off and his hand broke off,
We were having fun and his head flew off,
On the night the mummy came to the Hallowe'en party,
His bandages got caught on the door,
We opened the door and the mummy flew in,
On the night the mummy came to the Hallowe'en party.

*Deanne Peacock (8)*
*King Edward Junior School*

## S CLUB 7 CAME TO TEA

On the day S Club 7 came to tea,
They sang a song
All of them made mistakes,
Bradley sang the words wrong,
Jo made the music all funny,
Hannah and Rachel bumped into each other,
Paul slipped over and banged his head,
Tina and John got muddled up with the dance,
On the day S Club 7 came to tea.

*Chloe Chapman (8)*
*King Edward Junior School*

## THE DAY A MUMMY CAME TO TEA

On the day a mummy came to tea,
The mummy walked into the pond,
The mummy's leg got stuck down the loo,
The mummy tripped over the wire of the TV,
The mummy stuck his head down the loo
And flushed the toilet so he lost his head,
The mummy fell downstairs,
All because his head was bandaged up,
On the day a mummy came to tea.

*Lucy Melton  (7)*
*King Edward Junior School*

## THE DINOSAUR'S FIRST SCHOOLDAY

On the day a dinosaur came to school with me,
He started to eat my book for lunch,
The teacher said 'Get your other book.'
So I got it.
Halfway through,
The dinosaur spat on it.
Then there was a hole right through the book,
So I did not do any work all term.

*David Colwill  (8)*
*King Edward Junior School*

## AUTUMN

The crunchy leaves
Falling from the trees.
A twister of red and yellow,
Brown and orange leaves.
A tumble of leaves
Falling to the ground.
The conkers fall
In their spiky shells.
The crack that the conkers make
Makes you feel joyful.

*Louise Edgley (8)*
*King Edward Junior School*


## AUTUMN

In autumn, conkers are big.
Crackling leaves
Dancing to the ground.
When autumn comes again,
The leaves are different colours,
Red, orange, brown and yellow.
Shining conkers,
Children finding helicopters
From the sycamore trees.

*Jonathan Rigby (9)*
*King Edward Junior School*

## MY BOARD

My board is magic.
My board can talk.
My board is fun.
My board is cool.
My board is wicked.
My board can ride a motorbike.
My board is really, really *smart!*

*Declan Heady (7)*
*King Edward Junior School*


## BIRDS

Big birds,
Small birds,
Lovely birds,
Talking birds,
Singing birds,
I like all birds,
Lovely birds,
Foreign birds,
Chirping birds,
Nasty birds,
They're all lovely birds.

*Niomi Gill (8)*
*King Edward Junior School*

## WHY?

'I'm just going out with my friend'
'Why?'
'Because there's a disco!'
'Why?'
'Because it's Valentine's Day'
'Why?'
'Because it's the one day in the year
    when people love each other lots.'
'Why?'
'Please stop saying 'Why?'
'Why?'
'Because you're giving me a headache'
'Why?'
'I don't know why'
'Why?'

*Antonia Elise Butcher  (7)*
*King Edward Junior School*

## AUTUMN

Falling, crisping, dancing, swaying, brown and red leaves.
Leaves are falling, dancing and twisting.
Trees are swaying, flying and small.
Leaves are brown, red, yellow, green and orange.

*Kelly Long  (7)*
*King Edward Junior School*

## AUTUMN

Autumn is when conkers come.
They fall off trees,
They are spiky,
They have silk inside the shell.
When we pick them up
We crack the shell.
There's a conker inside!
There are leaves which are
 Red, yellow and brown.
They are crispy and crunchy,
Some have holes in them.

*Lee-Ann Watson  (7)*
*King Edward Junior School*


## MY PET

My pet is a zog and it gets into a terrible mog.
It runs around the house like a little mouse.
It jumps on the bed with its head, head, head.
It gulps its food.
My mum thinks it's rude!
I sold it for a pound
Then guess what I found?

*Leilani Rabemananjara  (8)*
*King Edward Junior School*

## AUTUMN

Autumn leaves are different colours.
Brown, yellow, orange and red.
They make a bed for the ground.
Autumn conkers are so much fun.
They are small and shiny
Like wooden marbles in the sun.
In autumn the grass is damp and jewelled.
The acorn shell is bumpy.
The leaves fall off the trees
And dance in the air.
They tumble and twist,
Twist and twist and sway
Autumn!

*Ross McQuaid (8)*
*King Edward Junior School*


## AUTUMN

Crispy, crunchy, crumbly leaves
Tumbling round and round.
The leaves are bright red
Like the big golden sun.
The grass is jewelled with dew.
Silk inside a chestnut shell.
The acorns are hard as merry fall.

*Emma Furness (8)*
*King Edward Junior School*

## WHY?

'I've got to take the dog out'
'Why?'
'Because it needs the toilet'
'Why?'
'Because it can't do it in the house!'
'Why?'
'Because it's house trained!'
'Why?'
'Won't you stop saying why?'
'What?'

*Geraldine Fleming  (7)*
*King Edward Junior School*


## MY MUM

My mum hums to songs
My mum hums to songs
What can I do what can I do?
I don't know what to do thank God
She might have the flu but she still sings
What can I do? What can I do?
She is always rude.

*Katie Richardson  (7)*
*King Edward Junior School*

## WITHOUT YOU

Without you
I'm like a heart without blood.
I'm like a train without tracks.
Without you.
I'm like a false alarm,
I'm like an eye without a tear,
Without you.
But whatever I do you always understand.
You'll always have the key to my heart.
The tissues to my eye.
The arm round my shoulder.
So whatever I do
I always know that
You will be there.

*Sarah Snow (11)*
*Manea Community Primary School*


## THE ICE CREAM MAN

When summer's in the country,
And the sun's a ray of heat,
The ice cream man with his van,
Goes driving down the lanes.

Beneath the roof of his van,
Oh, what a joyful sight,
To see him fill the cones,
With mounds of cooling pink or white.

Vanilla, chocolate, strawberry,
or chilly lollies to lick,
From packets full of juicy ice,
Green, orange, white or yellow.

*Tiffany Hollingsworth (10)*
*Manea Community Primary School*

# THE MOUTH

Mouths are long
and mouths are wide,
mouths have saliva
all inside.

Mouths have lips
which are usually pink,
except when you've
been sucking ink.

Mouths have teeth
that like gnashing food,
mouths make noises
that sound quite rude.

A tongue is the
strangest thing,
in your mouth
it lets you sing.

Mouths are rather
near your chin,
mouths are used to
smile and grin.

Above your mouth
is a nose,
muscles make mouths
go open, close.

*Luke Collet-Fenson  (10)*
*Mepal And Witcham School*

## BANANAS

I like the way their skins unzip,
In little cartoon strips,
They have no pips,
They are just like a squashy moon,
They have a smile,
But when you bite their heads off they don't!

*Emma Hayes  (9)*
*Mepal And Witcham School*


## KINDNESS

Kindness is yellow
It smells like honey
Kindness tastes like pancakes
it sounds like a person singing
It feels like a sponge
Kindness lives in your heart.

*Rory Martin  (9)*
*Mepal And Witcham School*


## HATE

Hate is horrible and black
Never has a smile on his face
hate lives in a dark land of mystery
Hate will get you if you're not careful
He's related to jealousy
Never been soft and cuddly.

*Christie Watson  (9)*
*Mepal And Witcham School*

## HOPE

It is red
Smells like melted chocolate
It tastes like chocolate and toffee
Softly talking
It feels soft and furry
Lives in your heart
It looks like a warm fire.

*Paul Goodman (10)*
*Mepal And Witcham School*


## DISAPPOINTMENT

Disappointment is dark blue and grey
Smells horrible like manure and smoke
Tasting sour like bitter lemon
Feeling hard and bumpy
Sounding mean, sad and hard
Living in mean humans.

*Leanne Cole (10)*
*Mepal And Witcham School*


## HARMONY

Harmony is as red, red as roses.
It smells of nice smelling perfume.
Tastes of jelly and ice cream.
It lives in the middle of your heart.
Sounds of playing harps
Looks like a very very beautiful lady.

*Gemma Chamberlain (10)*
*Mepal And Witcham School*

## WAR

War is bad.
it smells like gas.
War tastes like poisonous flies.
It sounds like gunfire.
War feels like scars and bullet holes.
It lives in a gun at the bottom of the volcano.

*Sam Smith (9)*
*Mepal And Witcham School*


## WAR

War is brown and greenish,
War smells like gunpowder,
War tastes like shrapnel,
War sounds like bang,
War feels sharp and spiky,
War lives in guns.

*Luke Baker (11)*
*Mepal And Witcham School*


## YOUTH

Youth is the colour of the rainbow.
It smells of sweetest golden honey.
The sweetest chocolate is youth.
The sound of the sweetest dove.
It gives the feeling of happiness and kindness
And it lives with you forever.

*Rose Elizabeth Rowell (9)*
*Mepal And Witcham School*

## How To Make A Rat

His tail like a worm which can squirm.
His eyes like two marbles, blood red.
His fur like a ton of lion's mane.
His teeth like little diamonds the shape of squares.
His legs like chewed pencils.
His claws like sharp pointed lead -
*Ready to chop off your head!*

*Blake Sanders  (9)*
*Mepal And Witcham School*


## My Old Teddy

I love you though your eyes are drooping,
I love you thought your paws are ripped to shreds,
I love you though your head is buried in the shed,
I love you though your fur is falling out,
I love you though your tail is torn,
I love you though your ears are cut,
I still love you old teddy.

*Andrew Horsfall  (8)*
*Mepal And Witcham School*


## Love

Love is kind, lovely and smells like flowers.
Love is pink, sounds friendly and tastes of strawberry.
Love feels soft, furry and lives inside your heart.

*Soffia Handley  (11)*
*Mepal And Witcham School*

## HAIR

Hair is blonde
Hair is brown
And hair can even be pink.

Hair is long
Hair is short
Not very many people have none.

Curly hair
Straight hair
And even sticking up hair.

Tied back
Left down
Put in pony tails.

Boys' hair
Girls' hair
On top of my head is my hair.

*Richard Day  (9)*
*Mepal And Witcham School*


## DEATH!

It is dark red
Smells like a rotting body
It tastes like blood
Sounds like sonic bombs
It feels like disease
Lives in the dark!
It looks like an alien.

*Daniel Duffy  (11)*
*Mepal And Witcham School*

## How To Make A Cat

She needs
A head like a soft tennis ball.
A tail like a piece of wool.
A leg like a walking stick that walks around.
A body like a soft lightweight to join on to the rest.
A pair of whiskers on each side like a white piece of silk.
A pair of glowing eyes like marbles.
A nose like a wet piece of rubber.
A mouth like a wet open gap.
A lot of fur like cotton.
That's how to make a cat miaow! Miaow!

*Jodi Leigh Rayner (8)*
*Mepal And Witcham School*


## Jealousy

Jealousy is the reddest thing alive
The smell is of sweet toilet cleaner
But I'd never even lick the surface
If you've ever swilled your mouth out
With a mixture of salt and water you know the taste
When you own jealousy it's so annoying
That's because it buzzes all the time
The texture's really rather rough but a little wet
Dry musty places, near people of course
Is where the big foaming slug-like creature lives.

*Syringa Fox (11)*
*Mepal And Witcham School*

## IF YOU WANT TO SEE A TIGER

If you want to see a tiger,
You must go down to the soggy, muddy, end of the jungle.
I know a tiger who lives down there,
he's a mean, he's a fast, he's a hungry, he's a huge,
Yes if you really want to see a tiger,
You must go down to the soggy, muddy, end of the jungle.
Go down gently to the end of the jungle and say,
Tiger papa,
Tiger papa,
Tiger papaaa.
Out he'll come,
Don't stick around,
*'Run for your life!'*

*Krystal Sturman  (8)*
*Mepal And Witcham School*


## HOW TO MAKE A CHIMPANZEE

He needs
Some hands like us,
Some feet like hands,
A head like an ape,
A torso from a human,
Some fur like an orang-utan,
And finally the disgusting part
Some insides like a human.

*Ben Somers  (8)*
*Mepal And Witcham School*

## THE MAGIC SCHOOL BOARD

The day had come,
The classroom would be finished,
The board arrived but nobody knew its secret.

A little girl called Lucy-May
Wrote upon the board one day
A story about a pirate named Red Beard
And to the school's surprise appeared,
A pirate ship sailing by,
And a beautiful parrot in the sky.
Who could they belong to?

Lucy-May thought she knew
Exactly what to do.
She drew a picture of herself in pirate gear
And suddenly lost all her fear.
Next she knew she was on the boat,
But Red Beard got her by the throat.

The littlest boy of all
Ran back in school
And drew on the board
A picture of a cutlass sword.
Red Beard turned to see the lad,
Lucy-May was rather glad.

Lucy and Red Beard started fighting,
The scene they set was very frightening!
Lucy-May eventually won!

But how would they get rid of the ship?
Suddenly a puff of smoke appeared on top of the pond
The teacher had rubbed it out,
So that's the little secret!

*Amber Rutterford (8)*
*Mepal And Witcham School*

## TO TRACY MY DEAD PET GUINEA PIG

I still love you though you were old and lazy,
I still love you though your eyes were hazy,
I still love you though your squeak was hoarse,
I still love you though your legs were stiff,
I still love you though your fur was matted,
I still love you though your ears were tattered,
I still love you though your claws were mouldy,
I still love you though your teeth were sharp,
I love you, yes, I love you, Tracy mine!

*Charlotte Collet-Fenson (8)*
*Mepal And Witcham School*


## I LOVE BLUE TED

I love his ears because they are fluffy and small.
I love his fur because it's blue and deep and silky so I fall asleep.
I love his eyes because they are big, orange and round with black spots.
I love his growl because it's low and deep and comforting.
I love his legs because they are short and stubby with white paws.
I love his arms because they hug his body.
I love his red nose because it's wobbly and bent
                    And that's blue Ted.

*Alexandra Baldwin (9)*
*Mepal And Witcham School*

## TO MY OLD TEDDY BEAR SNEEZY

I still love you though your clothes are dirty and torn,
I still love you though your red nose is scratched,
I still love you though your fur is dirty,
I still love you though your hat is bent,
I still love you though your beans inside you are flat,
I still love you though your eyes aren't very bright,
I still love you though your ears are quite muddy,
I still love you though your tail has lost its beans,
I still love you though your fur is muddy and brown,
I love you, yes, I love you Sneezy mine!

*Nicola Housden  (9)*
*Mepal And Witcham School*


## TO MY BROTHER'S HAMSTER

I love you though you are underground.
I love you though you're dead.
I love you though you're not alive.
I love you though you're in a good place.
I love you though you're in Heaven.
I love you even if you are in hell.
I love you so much Fudge.

*Jordan Houghton  (8)*
*Mepal And Witcham School*

# A Dog Like A Dog

Two ears like flat fish,
A tail like a curly caterpillar,
A tongue like a pink leaf,
A nose like a black wet triangle,
A belly like some beef but it's hairy,
Paws like paws,
But most of all it's my *doggy!*

*Leanne Alice Jeffrey  (8)*
*Mepal And Witcham School*


# The Voyage

On my voyage I went to Mars I found a yellow skateboard
I rode up and down and round in one of the pits and away I soared

On my voyage I went to a place far away it was called the Milky Way.
I had a great play day with my friend Jim.

On my voyage I went to Germany and met a tramp called Bob.
I gave him a building job.

On my voyage I went to Bubblegum Town.
I met a man who was a circus clown.

On my voyage I had a trip on a ship across the Pacific Ocean.
There were lots of funny pirates on board who were very sick.

On my voyage I went to the sun.
When I landed I got burnt and shrivelled up.

*Philip E Bailey  (8)*
*Milton CE School*

## HALLOWE'EN

Hallowe'en is cool,
Some think it's scary,
It's cool because there
Are no fairies.

Tuesday is today,
So let's have some fun,
We will go trick or treating,
So are you going to come?

Why don't you come?
Don't lean
On the sofa,
It's Hallowe'en.

*Michael Ellum  (8)*
*Milton CE School*


## MY FRIEND

Chelsey is my best friend
And sometimes we pretend
That we are sisters

We like to swap our toys
And both hate the boys
They're noisy!

We'll always be together
Always forever
Chelsey is my friend.

*Ruby Weeks  (7)*
*Milton CE School*

## MY SEASIDE DREAM

My seaside dream
I love ice cream
The smell of the sea
Are those boats looking at me!
Donkey rides
Look!
Here comes the tide
I make castles with sand
All the shells go through my hand
The fish from the sea
I like for my tea
There are rock pools as well
Phew, what a smell!
The sea hits the rocks
So noisy flocks
The seagulls of course
Oh no an octopus
The sun is shining
Watch the fish dining
My dream finished there
Err, I will go down the stair.

*Hannah Hill  (7)*
*Milton CE School*


## CHILDREN

Children in the lounge
Children in the hall
Children on a postcard
Children big and small

Children hot
Children cool
Children on a photo
Children in a pool

Children English
Children French
Children at home
And children on the bench

Children on a boat
Children like fish
Children like food
All in a dish.

*Shona Forge  (7)*
*Milton CE School*


## THE MAN IN THE MOON

I look up to a star
I wonder how it got so far
It twinkles up in the sky
I just wonder why.

The star's friend is the moon
He lights up every afternoon
His shape changes throughout the weeks
Every day the strange man peeks.

The man in the moon is very old
I think he must be very cold
I would really love to walk on the moon
I hope I will one day soon.

*Jacob Wisbey  (8)*
*Milton CE School*

## CHRISTMAS FUN

We run down the stairs on Christmas morning
It is so early, the day is just dawning.

Let's look under the Christmas tree
Are there any presents for you and me?

The tree decorations sparkling with light
Shining on the presents wrapped up so tight.

We open our presents with closed eyes
Then we take a peek to see the surprise.

Thanks Father Christmas for stopping by
We hope you and the reindeer have a good fly.

*Thomas Western  (8)*
*Milton CE School*


## SAILING

Boats going fast,
Sailors racing not to be last.
Waves high,
Oh my!
As the sailors head for shore,
Waves roar.
There's the line,
Will the prize be mine?

*Emily McDonald  (8)*
*Milton CE School*

## A Pirate's Life For Me

If I were a pirate sailing the sea,
looking for the island that calls to me.
'Look for my treasure all buried here,
to find it, my friend, it may take a year.'
Days and days I'd sail on the sea,
looking for the island waiting for me.
With me wooden leg and pirate hat,
a patch on my eye, I'd have to look like that.
The perfect pirate, a cutlass by my side,
every baddie would run and hide.

Captain Jim is me name,
seeking fortune and fame.
I'd stand on the deck of my ship and say,
'The treasure is ours with luck today!'
Gold and jewels all waiting to be found,
buried in a chest deep in the ground.
My crew will help dig far and wide,
for the treasure trying to hide.
I love a pirate's life, it's for me,
the best way to sail the sea.

The treasure map is in my hand,
I hope that we soon find land.
The Jolly Roger flies so high,
it makes me proud and want to cry.
I am a good pirate, you see,
the treasure will help poor people in need.
There's a shout from the crow's nest up high,
Jack points to where the sea meets the sky,
I don't believe it,
'Land ahoy!'

*James Ostler (8)*
*Milton CE School*

## PEOPLE

When people stand and stare
To look at the bear
In a zoo
Waiting all day
To come out and play
They do not notice
The birds and animals
That live all around
And can be found
In their homes
Or in the ground.

*Emma Murphy (8)*
*Milton CE School*


## SPACE RACE

We are having a race
So we better get a pace
3
2
1
*Go!*

I am in first place
But it hurts round my waist
Maybe I should lose some weight
So I can beat my mate.

*Stephen Bargh (8)*
*Milton CE School*

## LIFE IS...

Life is something that
Will never stop living!
Our heart is what keeps us living.
What we do when we die
Is our souls carry on living!
We can live on and on.
Never dying, never gone.
Life is always here.

Life is something that
Will never stop living.
We can't stop ourselves from dying.
Death is just a part of life.
When we're gone we're gone.
Some people die young.
Some people die old.
Every day we're dying.

*Karen Cunningham (10)*
*Murrow Primary School*


## ANGER

Anger is red
It tastes like mould
It smells like a volcano
It feels like someone punching you
It hurts your feelings.

*Steven Lee (9)*
*Murrow Primary School*

## ANGER IS . . .

Anger is as red as blood,
It smells like a fire,
It tastes like hot curry,
It sounds like thunder,
It feels like roughness,
It hurts their feelings.
Anger is red,
It smells like acid,
It tastes like out of date yoghurt,
It sounds like a wall fall down,
It feels like a punch,
It hurts them.

*Andy Cunningham (10)*
*Murrow Primary School*


## DOGS

Dogs go woof woof
Dogs go woof woof
Dogs have a big wet nose
And they have tiny toes
Dogs have a tiny tum
When you say come
They lick your thumb
Dogs like to play with a shoelace
They also like to lick your face
I give my dog lots of food
My dog is called Gertrude.

*Emma Harris (9)*
*Murrow Primary School*

# As I

As I walk along the road,
I see a dog run past.
As I see the smiling faces,
I want to know how long it will last.

As I sit near the sea,
I watch the waves come near.
As I sieve the golden sand,
I hope no one is in fear.

As I sit on the bench,
I see some children run towards me.
As I watch them talk and laugh,
I fall asleep, and dream.

*Helen Halton  (10)*
*Murrow Primary School*


# Anger Is . . .

Anger is red just like a flame
A touch of petal to make it rain
Anger is the colour of blood
Anger is death
Anger smells like acid
Anger feels like a cold.

*Ashley Virgo  (9)*
*Murrow Primary School*

# As I ...

As I look around out here,
  I see all the sights that there is to see.
I watch the people walking round
  And the mini buses that come round.

As I sit and watch the sea,
  The waves come in and splash me.
I hear the whoosh and the splash
  And watch the boats bounce up and down.

As I sit and watch the children,
  They are having fun just playing there.
All they want to do is play,
  They can't just sit there all day.

Life cannot be still, not even for a minute,
  Half a minute, a second.

*Amy Morris  (10)*
*Murrow Primary School*


# ANIMALS

I am a little dog
I hop around like a frog
Bang bang my legs must go
When I play out in the snow.

I am a little cat
I climb about like a rat
Miaow miaow my voice must go
When I play out in the snow.

I am a little butterfly
I can fly to the sky
Flap flap my wings must go
When I play out in the snow.

I am a little fish
I'm going to be put on a dish.
Swish swish my fins go
When I don't play out in the snow.

*Petra Blackwell (10)*
*Murrow Primary School*


## LOVE

Love is
Floating in the air,
It's calling people everywhere
Always loving always warm.
We all have to fall in love,
But until then I am going to play.
Love is always coming.

Love is
Floating in the air,
It's calling people everywhere
We can't stop ourselves from loving,
It's like a lovely hot muffin
Some fall in love when they're young
And some are old.

*Zoe Hennells (9)*
*Murrow Primary School*

## THE NAUGHTY BOY

There once was a little boy,
Who always stayed up in his room,
And through the summer of moonlight,
He was cleaning away with the broom.
When his mother said there was a person she'd like to meet,
Her little boy who would say through the keyhole
Get me a sweet.
He would listen to his music,
He would watch his videos,
Because he's so naughty he'd suck his little toes.
His mum always calls him,
But he never answers.
He has his music on blast.
His mum calls him a dancer.

*Sarah Skinner  (9)*
*Murrow Primary School*


## PAIN

Pain is black
Pain tastes like grapefruit
Pain sounds like screams
Pain smells like gas
Pain feels like a knife
Pain lives in the brain.

*Lee Heath  (9)*
*Murrow Primary School*

## ANGER POEMS

Anger is red
It smells like mould
It tastes like hot water
It sounds like roaring
It feels hard and sharp
It lives inside you

Anger is pink
It smells like sweat
It tastes like a tiger
It sounds like bubbles
It feels like burning
It lives in the brain.

*Ashley Green  (9)*
*Murrow Primary School*


## HAPPINESS

The colour of happiness is rose pink.
Happiness tastes sweet.
Happiness smells of flowers in a meadow.
Happiness looks like friendship.
Happiness lives in our hearts.

*Craig Brown  (9)*
*Murrow Primary School*

## WHAT IS A PAINTING?

A painting is a frozen scene of colour,
That brings joy to lives.

It is a picture of a 1000 words,
Set in one.

It is hope and light,
Whether big or small.

It is a gateway to dreams,
For those who have none.

It is a picture to life and imagination,
Painted by one.

*Edward Middleton (11)*
*The Rackham CE Primary School*


## THE GALLOPING HORSE

The young black galloping horse,
Fifteen hands high precisely,
Flowing, strong and fast
Like a marathon runner,
A winner in every race.
Galloping for money and fun,
The young black galloping horse
Always wins the race.

*Lucie Potter (10)*
*The Rackham CE Primary School*

# THE TINY DAISY

The tiny daisy
Only eight days old
Young, lively and fun.
Dancing in the sunlight,
Sleeping in the moonlight.
It makes me feel huge
Like a branch of a tree.
The tiny daisy
Reminds us of how long
Life can be.

*Jennifer Ludman  (11)*
*The Rackham CE Primary School*

# THE SNOWMAN

The fat snowman
That will only last till the sun comes out
White, frozen and alone
Cracking its twiggy fingers
Moving its long nose in the wind
It makes me feel happy
Like a sun with a smile
The fat snowman
It's winter time, cold and chilly.

*Rachel Seymour  (10)*
*The Rackham CE Primary School*

## A BOOK

A book is merely a piece of paper - but only at first sight -
It is a porthole to another dimension,
Let it take you on its flight.

The black and white writing will suddenly form -
A picture in your head -
The book's pictures will not be revealed -
Until its adventurous pages are read.

You can hear the voices in your mind,
While characters shout out in glee,
You can remember books dearly,
In your past life history.

Whether your book is romance or fun,
When you don't read it you're sad.
The end in my opinion is as quick as a hare -
The worst bit is the end - it's bad!

A book is a person if you let it be,
It is its characters inside,
It is everything you want it to be -
It is a shark ready to open its jaws

And it's especially for me!

*Lynsey Jones  (10)*
*The Rackham CE Primary School*

## SCHOOL DAYS

Monday is a school day -
We start assembly where we pray -
At the end of the day -
'Okay, it's home time,' the teacher will say.

Today is Tuesday, a school day,
We walk to school all the way,
The lessons go on all through the day -
At the end of school we have tried as we may.

Wednesday is the middle of the week,
At playtime we play hide and seek,
When in class - to others we must not speak
We have only got two days left in this week.

Come Thursday, goody art club tonight
I'll be trying with all my might -
To get this project right -
And tonight my brother and I will have less time to fight!

Hooray hooray, it's Friday today
Last day at school I'll say -
I'll play with my friends if I may -
And Saturday and Sunday are not school days.

*Natalie Szulc (9)*
*The Rackham CE Primary School*

## THE LONELY CHRISTMAS TREE

The lonely Christmas tree,
Always locked up in the loft,
Dusty, cold, green,
Spiky thumb,
Like cocktail sticks, stuck into your thumb,
Putting on the decorations, what a lovely feeling,
Your birthday has already come,
The lonely Christmas tree
Is now a happy tree,
Down with you.

*Sabrina Woollard  (9)*
*The Rackham CE Primary School*

## THE MIDNIGHT PUSS

The midnight puss
Its eyes glow as the night enters,
Pouncing, darting, running
A wild beast roaming the streets
An animal, an amazing land where felines run free,
it makes me feel like a spy watching a tiger,
The midnight puss,
Reminds me how our lives can be so more interesting!

*Katharine Hardman  (9)*
*The Rackham CE Primary School*

## THE STAR

The sparkling star
Been around for millions of years
Glittering, twinkling, shining
It points to where you should go
It smiles in children's dreams
It makes me feel weak
Like a fish without a backbone
The sparkling star
Reminds us that we can shine too.

*Ashleigh Witt (11)*
*The Rackham CE Primary School*

## A STOUT TREE

A stout tree
Grows in forests
Bulgy, rough, spiky,
Their branches swing side to side,
Like a person swishing their hair
Makes me feel like a tiny mouse
A stout tree
It reminds us how lucky we are.

*Emily Richardson (9)*
*The Rackham CE Primary School*

## KITTENS

Kittens here kittens there,
Running, crawling everywhere,
Jumping out they'll give you a scare!
He plays with toys though doesn't share,
He scratches here and scratches there,
'Aw!' 'Oh!' 'No, no!' Not over there!
Sleeping on the front door mat,
Here they spy a sleepy rat,
Prancing, catching all of the day,
Sleepy rat please wake up and run away,
Gobbling up their milk so quick,
Slurping up their milk so slick,
'Lick lick lick,'
I really think it's time for bed,
'Night, night sleepy head.'

*Anna Wallis & Katharine Hardman (10)*
*The Rackham CE Primary School*


## THE SAD SNOWMAN

The sad snowman
Built by the young little boy
White, cold, lonely
Like a toddler without its parents and friends
The sad snowman
It makes me feel small and lonely.

*Jacqueline Hedges (10)*
*The Rackham CE Primary School*

## A BRIGHT STAR

A bright star
That shines very bright,
Bright, gold and old
Like a diamond floating in the sky,
Reaching into space so high,
I feel young
Like a baby that has just been born
A bright star
Reminds us how pretty the sky can be.

*Catherine Ascough  (10)*
*The Rackham CE Primary School*


## THE MOON

The shiny moon
Been in Heaven for thousands of years
Sparkly, glittery and silver
It's an eye waiting to blink
And it dances around the world.
It makes me feel warm
Like a worm in the earth
The shiny moon
Makes you feel old.

*Chantle Oakes  (10)*
*The Rackham CE Primary School*

## THE STARS

The sparkling stars,
They are there every night.
Gold, glittering, crystallised
Like a finger pointing,
Like an eye, when it sparkles.
It makes me feel so low,
So low like a tiny ant,
The sparkling stars
Reminds us how old we are.

*Jade Whitmore  (10)*
*The Rackham CE Primary School*

## THE CUDDLY FERRET

The cuddly ferret,
Descending from the mongoose
Friendly, fun and funny
Eating like a starving mouse,
Trotting like a horse
The ferret makes me feel happy and joyful
The cuddly ferret
Reminds us how happy we are on earth.

*Chloe Elms  (10)*
*The Rackham CE Primary School*

## THE ENORMOUS SPHINX

The enormous sphinx
With a human's head on top.
Huge, mountain structure
An alive lion staring at you
A structure waiting to leap at you
Makes me feel a little boy being chased
Makes me feel a target of prey
The enormous sphinx
Reminds us of how lucky we are.

*Matthew Parish  (10)*
*The Rackham CE Primary School*


## THE TINY RAINDROP

The tiny raindrop
Puffed from a fluffy cloud
Small, wet, cold.
A small drop of colour spat from Heaven,
A tear falling from a cloud's eye.
It makes me feel strong
Like I'm not alone.
It makes me feel lucky, that I've got a home.

*Lucy Kinna  (9)*
*The Rackham CE Primary School*

## WATER

The icy water
A mixture of solids and liquids
Refreshing, clear and relaxing
It massages your body
As if it were real hands
It makes me feel sleepy and calm
It's like a deserted desert
The icy water
The crisp and clear mirror and only disturbed
By the infrequent ripples.

*Roger Goetze (11)*
*The Rackham CE Primary School*


## THE ENORMOUS SKYSCRAPER

The enormous skyscraper
Seventy years old
Strong, mighty, gigantic.
Titanic reaching to the clouds,
Like an arm pointing to space,
Makes me feel small,
Like a caterpillar that no one notices,
The enormous skyscraper,
Reminds us of how small we are.

*Hayden Watson-Stewart (10)*
*The Rackham CE Primary School*

## VOLCANO

The erupting volcano
Spreads out across the street,
Seeking, hunting, searching,
The tongue slurping out of the gigantic mouth,
Makes me feel as if I am burning inside.
Like a fire blaring in the heart of me,
The erupting volcano
The destruction makes me think
Of what the world might come to!

*Emmeline Holt (11)*
*The Rackham CE Primary School*


## MY SCHOOL

M others waiting at the gate
Y ellow busy books everywhere

S miling teachers helping you along
C hildren playing with their friends
H istory lessons are the best
O pen doors to welcome you in
O ff we go to the big playground passing infants on the way
L earning a new thing every day.

*Jake Caffrey (11)*
*The Rackham CE Primary School*

## THE DRAGON

D ark, scaly skin covers its body
R ed hot flames build up in its mouth
A n angry scowl beams at unwary passers-by
G green claws, gnashing jaws rage at intruders
O n a rock by the cliffs he perches in a cave
N ight-time he comes out to play.

*Michael Chapman  (11)*
*The Rackham CE Primary School*


## BODY PARTS

The head is shaped like an upside-down dustbin,
The eyes are like bouncy balls,
A nose all big and pointy,
Our ears are always twitching
And mouths always smiling.

Shoulders like big, bold blades,
Leading to arms always dancing,
Down to elbows to protect us from a fall,
And hands to keep our fingers together,
Fingers that keep on moving.

Hips all strong and powerful
Keeping our legs running.
Our knees bony and knobbly.
Helping our legs to bend.
Feet keep us with the beat
Tapping along.
Toes to wriggle in the sand at the beach.

*Joshua Blyth  (9)*
*The Weatheralls Primary School*

# PARADISE ISLAND

When I am feeling sad and lonely
I dream of this one place;
The sun beats down on the golden beach,
The sand runs straight through my hands,
The waves keep me refreshed and so cool,
The palm trees shade my view from the sun,
Gleaming high in the sky,
Little oysters sit like statues on the ocean bed,
Schools of fishes glide through the ocean
Like clouds which bob in the sky.
I lie on the beach in my bright pink bathing suit,
Butlers waiting on me hand and foot,
Drinking exotic cocktails,
Little umbrellas propped in the top,
Vodka, Sangria and rum.
As the ice on my forehead melts to make me cool,
My hair lies flat on the beach,
Long, flowing and soft.
Then I wake up back to reality,
I realise just this,
That it is only a place I can dream of,
A figment of my imagination,
But sometimes I wish it were more!

*Rebecca Blyth  (11)*
*The Weatheralls Primary School*